MAKING

MEMORY BOOKS
&
JOURNALS

BY HAND

MAKING
MEMORY BOOKS
&
JOURNALS
BY HAND

42 projects for creatively recording your thoughts and memories

THUNDER BAY
P·R·E·S·S

First published in 2001 by

Thunder Bay Press

An imprint of the Advantage Publishers Group

5880 Oberlin Drive, San Diego, CA 92121-4794

www.advantagebooksonline.com

The work in this book originally appeared (in slightly different form) in *Making
Memory Books by Hand,* by Kristina Feliciano, *Making Journals by Hand,* by Jason
Thompson, and *Making Memory Boxes,* by Barbara Mauriello. Grateful acknowledg-
ment is given to Kristina Feliciano, Jason Thompson, and Barbara
Mauriello for permission to reprint their work in this special edition.

Work on pages 12-13, 18-115 originally appeared in:
Making Memory Books by Hand, 22 Projects to Make, Keep, and Share
By Kristina Feliciano
Design: The Design Company
Layout: SYP Design & Production
All photography by Kevin Thomas

Work on pages 14-15, 184-285 originally appeared in:
Making Journals by Hand, 20 Creative Projects for Keeping Your Thoughts
By Jason Thompson
Design: Lynn Faitelson
All photography by Kevin Thomas
"Choosing Your Paper" (see pages 14-15), by Megan
Fitzpatrick, originally appeared in the magazine *Personal
Journaling,* from F&W Publications. For more information
on this magazine, call 1-800-289-0963 or visit
www.journalingmagazine.com.

Work on pages 116-183, 286-293 originally appeared in:
Making Memory Boxes, Box Projects to Make, Give, and Keep
By Barbara Mauriello
Design: Lynn Faitelson

ISBN 1-57145-624-4

Printed in China.

10 9 8 7 6 5 4 3 2

CONTENTS

INTRODUCTION

The beautiful crafts in these pages originally appeared (in slightly different form) in the volumes *Making Journals by Hand* by Jason Thompson, *Making Memory Boxes* by Barbara Mauriello, and *Making Memory Books by Hand* by Kristina Feliciano. The overwhelming popularity and passion for memory-making crafts inspired this grand collection. Never before presented as a single volume, here is the wonderful work from all three volumes gathered together for creative memory-making inspiration.

Packed with journals, sketchbooks, travel diaries, photo and wedding albums, memory boxes, and portfolios, each section of this book is an exploration into the world of memory-making possibilities. Whether you enjoy sketching, scrap booking, creative collage, journaling, or simply collecting precious keepsakes, these projects are just for you. So get your scissors, grab the glue, unearth the pretty papers you've been saving, and enjoy the book!

JASON THOMPSON ON JOURNALING:

You are holding one of the first books of its kind to showcase the personal journals of writers, artists, and creative types. Among these pages you will find examples of daily journals, artists' sketchbooks, travel journals, historical journals, and more, dating from the middle eighteenth century to the present day. You will also find journal-keeping lessons and projects to follow along with.

Faithfully keeping a journal is an art, a craft, a discipline, a ritual, and, for many journal keepers, a release—a conduit for the ideas, inspiration, experiences, and dreams that flow in and out of our daily lives. The techniques vary, but the inspiration is universal. The daily process for many journalers is a way to say those things that don't get said in every day life. The insight we experience in quiet moments can gain strength and permanence when put to page. Our personal communication can lead to growth, change, and self-awareness, or just as importantly, simply serve as a memory of a time and place to look back to later on in life.

(from *Making Journals by Hand,* Introduction, copyright Rockport Publishers, 2000)

KRISTINA FELICIANO ON MEMORY BOOKS:

Stronger than a string of diary entries, more powerful than your average photo album, able to recall a long-ago experience with a single page, memory books just might be the finest way to celebrate all you hold dear. It's no wonder they have become so popular.

And one of the best things about memory books is that anyone can make one. We've all got our memories, our snapshots, our mementos—these and a basic understanding of bookmaking are all you need. How far you choose to go with your memory book is entirely up to you. Be sure to enjoy this artistic freedom. So many art forms are burdened with rules and with concerns about marketability. These are not the worries of people who make memory books. This is a very personal craft. That means whatever direction you go in with your book is the right one. You have only yourself and your memory to satisfy.

(from *Making Memory Books by Hand,*
Introduction, copyright Rockport Publishers, 2000)

BARBARA MAURIELLO ON MEMORY BOXES:

Anyone who has ever filled a shoebox with family photos or crammed small treasures into a cigar box has already made a memory box. Without having quite defined it before, we know exactly what it is. We also know that as we go through life squirreling away letters, seashells, report cards, broken watches, snippets of baby hair, and all of the ephemera of belonging, these boxes contain the core of a life. Memory boxes are projects that make the container as special as its contents.

However varied their design, most boxes share basic architectural elements. A case, a tray, a lid, and a flap-four units, and at least 400 ways to multiply, divide, and join them to create unique objects of beauty, whimsy, and practicality. Here is the heartening fact about boxmaking: Boxes do not become more difficult as you proceed from one style to another; they simply become either more like or less like each other. By the time you have completed one of each component—a tray, a case, a lid, and a flap—you will know all there is to know about the fundamentals of boxmaking. Then you can start to have fun.

(from *Making Memory Boxes,*
Introduction, copyright Rockport Publishers, 2000)

Basics

About Paper

When selecting specific papers for a project, ask yourself the following questions: Is the paper appropriate for the book's purpose? Does the paper help express the look or feel you want your book to have? Does the paper complement the other materials used in the book? Finally, ask the people working at paper stores and art stores for advice. They are usually quite knowledgeable and will be glad to help.

While modern technology has made it possible to produce mass quantities of paper cheaply, there are still papers being made around the world by hand using natural fibers and old-world techniques. These decorative papers work well as covers, end sheets, or even interior pages. A visit to a local paper store or a well-stocked art store will reveal the tremendous assortment of papers you can choose from. They can be thin enough to see through, such as many Japanese rice papers, or as thick as the cardboard of a corrugated box. They can be as smooth as silk tissue paper or as rough as tree bark.

All paper has one common characteristic—the grain. The grain indicates the arrangement or direction of the fibers. A book will be stronger, less likely to warp, and easier to fold if the grain of all your papers is parallel with the spine. Companies often label which way the grain runs. For machine-made commercial paper, the

grain usually runs the length of the paper. If the grain is not listed, you can test it by bending or folding the paper. A piece of paper folds easily and without cracking if the crease is parallel with the grain. If you fold a piece of paper and it shows signs of cracking along the crease, you know the grain runs in the opposite direction. If you still cannot determine which way the grain runs, cut a small piece and wet it. As the paper dries, it will begin to bend in the direction of the grain. For handmade papers, the grain is of less concern. It is arranged in many different directions, and is therefore not as clearly defined as in machine-made commercial paper.

Choosing Your Paper

All paper is not created equal. Yes, you could write in 39¢ school notebooks, but your journal should be recorded on a medium that will endure. Before you go out and buy reams of paper or a bound book of blank pages for your journal, try this inexpensive and relatively quick experiment to evaluate paper quality: Collect the morning paper from your front step (or neighbor's bushes, as the case may be), and after you've read it, leave a page sitting in direct sunlight. By dinner time, that page will already be yellowing, and you will have found that not all paper is meant to last. Up until the mid 1800s, paper was composed of cellulose fiber derived from old rags and linen, and bleached with lime, which is highly alkaline. The lime also served as a buffering agent, protecting the paper from external acid introduction, such as handling by human hands. But by the Civil War, the demand for paper out-stripped the supply of linen and rags, and new ingredients for paper-making had to be found.

The main ingredient in most modern paper is wood pulp, and the processes developed for bleaching, sizing (which waterproofs the paper to some extent to keep ink from bleeding) and finishing this paper involves a lot of highly acidic chemicals, which cause the paper to break down over time. This is why all those paperback books from your childhood are now falling apart. And the more you handled them; the more acid you introduced through the oils in your skin, further causing deterioration.

THE RIGHT STUFF

The main thing to look for when selecting paper for your journal is acid-free paper. Fifteen years ago, it was hard to find high-quality acid-free writing paper, but now almost every decent bookstore carries at least a few bound blank books of acid-free pages. These may cost a few dollars more than the acidic variety, but if you want people to be able to read your words in the future, it's worth the investment. Plus, to further assuage your guilt over spending the extra money, the processes used in producing acid-free paper are more environmentally friendly. Manufacturing acid-free paper produces fewer run-off contaminants, and the product usually includes some recycled content. If you prefer to

write at your computer, acid-free printer paper is also available. But remember to print your pages from time to time. After all, in a few more years, floppy disks may be museum pieces! For more information and sources on where to find archival products such as acid-free paper and journals, see the Resources section at the end of this book.

PRESERVATION NO-NO'S

Even if the paper you're using is of the best quality, acid and other destructive factors can be introduced inadvertently. Glue, binding cloth, staples and threads commonly used to hold books together can have disastrous effects on the longevity of your work. While there may not be too much you can do about these bad influences, here are some things you can easily avoid.

CLIPPINGS: Try to avoid introducing newspaper clippings into your journal pages, as the acid will migrate from the low-quality newsprint to your relatively expensive, high-quality pages, making it money ill-spent. Instead, copy clippings onto acid-free paper.

ACCESSORIES: Avoid using paper clips, rubber bands and self-adhesive notes as they can cause permanent damage to your pages. Even most inks can introduce harmful acid onto your paper, although for a small investment, you can buy ballpoint pens with acid-free inks.

OTHER DETRIMENTS: Light (especially UV), animals (including mice, cockroaches, silverfish, bookworms and your dog), food and drink, heat above 70 degrees (60 is safer, but rather limiting), and humidity are all environmental factors destructive to paper.

AVOIDING DAMAGE

If your goal is to make your writing last, even the right combination of paper, binding materials and ink alone won't preserve your journal for future generations. The manner in which you treat your journal also contributes to its longevity. Don't fold the page corners over to mark your place and don't use the book as a coaster for your morning coffee. Don't write in the bathtub (at least, don't write in the journal you want to save in the bathtub). Finally, once you've completed a volume, store it in a cool, dark dry place that is easy to clean... and (we hate to say it) clean there once in awhile. The best way to store your completed volumes is to keep them in archival quality (acid-free) boxes. Don't keep them in wooden chests as the chests can become infested, or in metal boxes, unless they're specially made for archival storage, as the boxes may corrode.

MAKING MEMORY BOOKS BY HAND

Materials and Supplies

In addition to various kinds of paper, there are a few
other materials and supplies needed to complete the
projects in this book.

Cloth

Most books use cloth for all or part of the cover. Binder's
cloth is a strong, durable cloth with a paper backing. It
can be purchased at binderies and paper stores. Other
types of cloth can also be used. If the cloth you want has a
loose weave or is very thin, it must be backed with paper
to give it added strength and provide a surface on which
to spread glue. Rice paper makes good backing material.

Adhesives

Cloth and paper are adhered to a book using glue or paste.
For the projects described in this book, polyvinyl acetate
(PVA) is recommended. It is white, dries clear, and can be
thinned with water. You can substitute PVA with other
white paper glues. You can also use wheat paste, rice paste,
or paste made from cornstarch. To mix your own paste,
look for recipe books that show you how.

Thread

The binding on some of the projects in this book is sewn.
Professional binders use linen thread, which is strong but
rather expensive. As a substitute, use thick cotton thread,
embroidery silk, or even dental floss if the book is small. A
variety of ribbons, cords, or twine can add color to your
spine. Avoid using sewing thread, which breaks easily.

Cover Board or Binder's Board

The front and back covers of most books are made with heavy paper or cardboard. Davy board, a type of cover board used by binders, can be purchased from local binderies or through catalogs. Cover boards vary in thickness from 0.02 inch (a thin board) to 0.147 inch (a thick board). The latter is almost impossible to cut by hand. For practical purposes, the thickness of the cover boards should be about 0.08 or 0.09 inch, except in cases when a thin board, such as shirt board (0.02), is required.

Scrap Paper

Making books by hand can get a bit messy. Use large scraps of paper as a barrier to protect your materials and work surface while gluing and cutting. Remember to discard wet barriers and replace them with clean, dry ones. Rolls of wax paper and craft paper wrappers are an inexpensive source of protective paper.

Sandpaper

Medium sandpaper can be used to round any sharp corners or irregular edges of your cover boards.

Damp Cloth

Keep a damp cloth handy while gluing. Use it to clean sticky fingers so that you do not get any unwanted glue on finished surfaces.

Tools

This list includes many of the tools needed to complete the projects in this book. Not every tool listed here is required for every project, of course. Some of the projects may require additional tools—such as a letterpress, electric drill, or a computer.

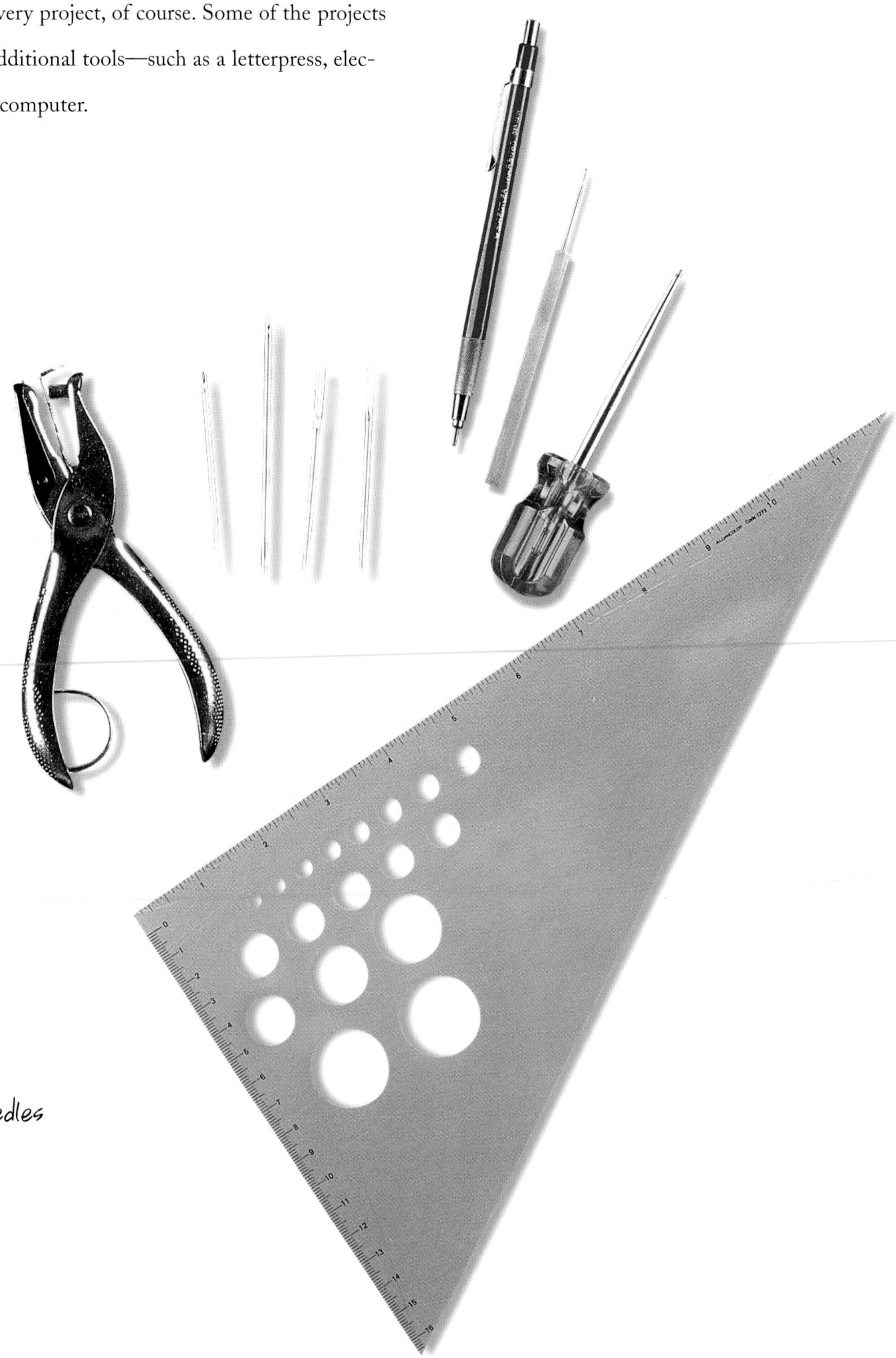

Square angle rule

Assorted craft needles

Pencil

Hole punch

Needle tool

Awl

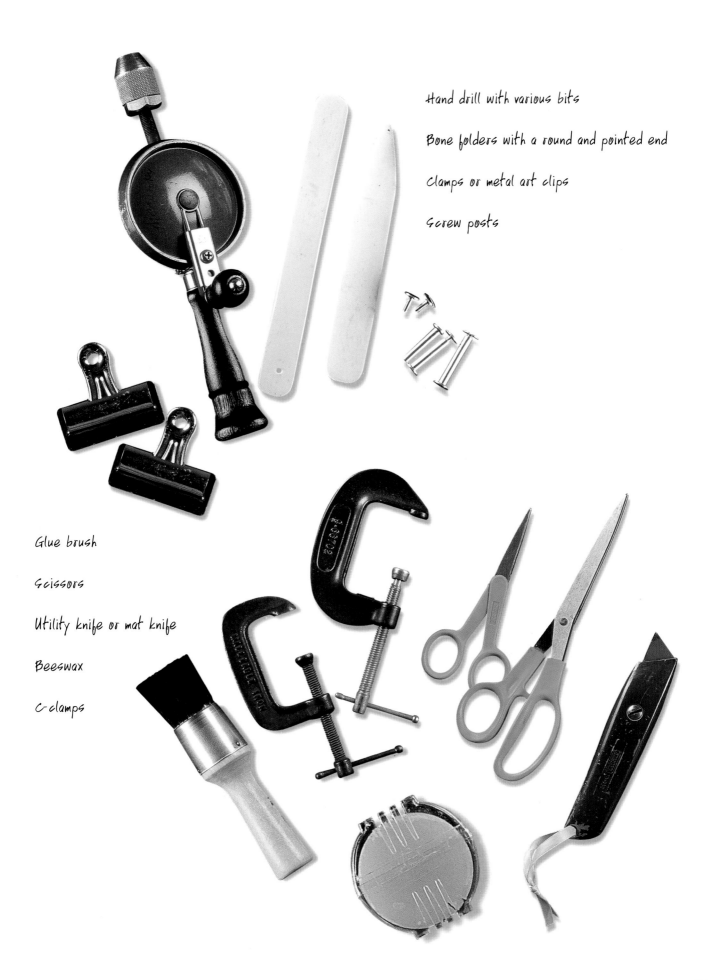

Hand drill with various bits

Bone folders with a round and pointed end

Clamps or metal art clips

Screw posts

Glue brush

Scissors

Utility knife or mat knife

Beeswax

C-clamps

How to Make Corners

For many of the projects in this book, cover boards are wrapped with either cloth or paper. As it requires practice to make neat corners, take time to study the three methods of wrapping corners described below. For each method, make sure you cut the material no closer than 1/4" (.5 cm) to the corners of the board.

Method One: For Thin Paper or Cloth

Cut off the corners of your material at a diagonal fold, and glue one side of the material down on the board.

Use a bone folder to press the paper down at a slight angle over the corner.

Glue and fold the paper on the adjacent side in the same way.

Method Two: For Thick or Brittle Paper

Cut off the corners of your paper at a diagonal fold, and glue one side down on the board. Then, with scissors, cut a straight line from the fold of the cloth that extends to the corner of the board.

With a bone folder or a finger, tuck the small triangular piece you have just created around the corner onto the lip of the adjacent side. Snip off the peak that has formed with scissors as shown.

Glue and fold the adjacent side down on the board.

 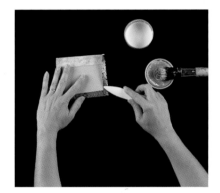

Method Three: For Cloth or Paper

Cut a square into the cloth or paper as shown. Cut carefully so that one corner of the square remains attached to the material.

Glue and fold the square over the inside of the board.

Glue and fold the adjacent sides of the material down on the inside of the board.

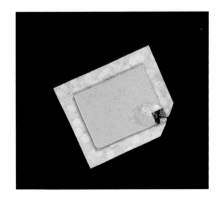 

travel memory books

OTHER PLACES, OTHER VIEWS

It's amazing the things that can be collected from a vacation: postcards, brochures, ticket stubs. It's the kind of stuff that usually winds up in a shoe box shoved somewhere in the far corners of the closet. Why not sort through that box and use the best of the lot in a memory book?

Or maybe you're a traveler of the armchair variety. There's a destination dear to your heart, so you make a travel book all about the place.

And let's not forget the travel diary, a type of memory book notable for its spontaneity. In it you can note your impressions, make sketches, and paste local headlines.

ected by an additional burden:
outhern belle mystique,
ften isolated by the size of
ces between homes.
learned well how to survive.
ever, may scare cowboys.

French Travelogue

BASED ON A PROJECT BY PETER MADDEN

"**A** book is a journey, and I almost always make my journeys into books," says artist Peter Madden, whose passion for travelogues was handed down from his mother (she kept meticulous scrapbook journals of every trip the family took for over twenty years). When he travels, Madden tries to keep an open mind about what he might collect for his book, absorbing, assimilating, collecting, roaming, and recording what he sees in photographs, sketches, and notes. What he winds up with might just look like a pile of junk—maps, postcards, rubbings, ticket stubs, newspaper clippings, and so on—but he edits it down to create richly evocative books whose every detail captures the essence of the place and his time there.

What You Need

Thin-gauge pine or plywood

Copper

Nails

Hammer

Saw

Drill

Nuts and bolts

Cardboard template

Brass hinges

Wood stain

Photocopies of mementos and solvent

Stamp made from an old cork

Almost bought the farm on the road between Nice and Monaco...

step-by-step

1. Making the covers

Begin by making a cardboard template the size of the book, to get a sense of what the book will eventually look like and to scale the pages. Cut the front and back covers, and the spine strip (which you can estimate by eye). The cover of Madden's book, for example, is 7 3/4" x 10 1/2" (19.5 cm x 27 cm), so he cut a spine strip that is 3/4" (2 cm) wide, which worked aesthetically and gave him enough room to fill the pages as planned.

2. Decorating the covers

Next, decorate the cover of the book and glue endpapers to the inside of both covers. To decorate his book, Madden transferred a rubbing of an old embossed leather book cover that he found at a flea market in Paris onto the wooden cover and stained it lightly to give it an antique look. On the inside of the wooden cover he glued handmade endpapers that he decorated with a handmade stamp—a bottle cork that he cut into a simple shape.

3. Aging and installing the hinges

Once the front and back covers have been decorated inside and out, hinge them to the spine strip using little brass hinges from the hardware store. Madden aged the hinges by oxidizing them with ammonia to darken and stain them. He then added copper stripping to the edges of the covers for a more finished look.

4. Filling the pages

Using solvent transfers is Madden's favorite method of adding content to his books. In this case, he made transfers from rubbings (also known as frottage) taken from textured buildings or signs where he vacationed. When the content of the book is finished, use rubber bands to hold the pages and covers in place while drilling the two holes necessary to bolt the book together.

5. Binding

Countersink the nuts and bolts in the two holes that have been drilled through the entire package: front cover, entire block of pages, and back cover. Madden then covered the holes with small diamond shapes cut from oxidized copper and nailed to the spine strip.

Variation
GREECE BOOK

10" x 8 ½" (25 cm x 22 cm)

For a slightly more organic look, Madden actually sewed through the binding, rather than using nuts and bolts. The found objects dangling from the spine—cherry pits, keys, religious medals, and sea shells—enhance the book's immediacy.

Guatemala Trip Journal

BASED ON A PROJECT BY LAURA BLACKLOW

Artist Laura Blacklow uses very little manipulation in her travel books. Rather than make color copies of her snapshots, for example, she uses the actual snapshots. The result is a book that feels entirely personal; a shoe box of memories made into book form. This is not to say that she doesn't pay attention to the book's aesthetics. She fusses over paper selection and is mindful of the juxtaposition of images: A page of Polaroids may face a full-page sketch, or pictures may be arranged into a panorama, as in this book, *Guatemala Trip Journal.* But her travel books themselves are slightly rough-hewn, as if they've been around.

What You Need

Medium-weight acid-free paper for pages

Heavyweight acid-free paper for cover

Ruler

Single-edge razor blade or stencil knife

Four thick, large rubber bands

Scissors

Bone folder

90-degree right triangle

PVA glue

step-by-step

1. Making the pages

Working with acid-free paper (acid can react with the chemicals in a photograph and result in yellowing and staining), mark off pages measuring 5 $\frac{1}{2}$" x 9 $\frac{3}{4}$" (14 cm x 24.5 cm), adding a $\frac{1}{2}$" (1 cm) to the binding edge only. Score the pages lightly with a utility knife and fold each page at the $\frac{1}{2}$" (1 cm) mark at the binding edge. This tab allows you to include Polaroids and other items of reasonable thickness in the book without preventing it from closing flat.

2. Making a pocket page

To measure for the height of the pocket page, double the height of the other pages, then subtract $\frac{1}{4}$" (.5 cm) so that it is the same height as the other pages but slightly lower in front where the mementos will be inserted. The pocket page is the same width as the other pages—with $\frac{1}{2}$" (1 cm) included for the spine and another $\frac{1}{2}$" (1 cm) added to the right side of the page for the seam of the pocket. Cut a small triangle at the bottom right corner and a small rectangle at the top right corner to create tabs to form the pocket. These tabs can be eliminated to create a page that folds down into the book.

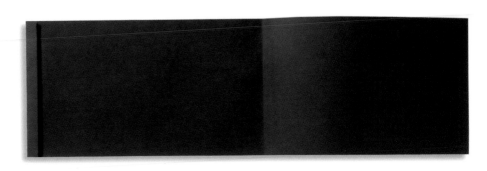

3. Making a fold-out page

Blacklow also made a fold-out page in black for a panorama consisting of Polaroids she took of the landscape. To make a fold-out page, cut a piece of paper twice as long as a single page minus 1" (3 cm)—not forgetting to add the $\frac{1}{2}$" (1 cm)—necessary for the binding side—so that it can fold in without interfering with the binding.

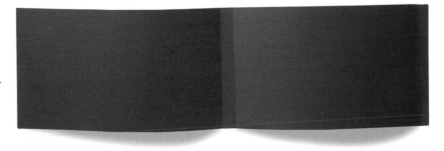

4. Cutting the cover

Cut the cover, which should be of heavier paper than the inside pages, 1/8" (.3 cm) larger than the inside pages to protect them. Score the folds for binding.

5. Binding

Stack the pages, taking care to line up all the tabs, and use heavy rubber bands to hold the stack together. Put the stacked pages into the cover and measure out five evenly spaced holes (these can be made with an electric or hand drill). Sew the binding (Blacklow used gold embroidery thread), starting at the center and working your way back.

Variation
SOUTHWEST TERRITORIES

7 ¼" x 8" (18.5 cm x 20 cm)

The signatures of Blacklow's book about her travels in the Southwest are similar in construction to those of the *Guatemala Trip Journal,* but the binding is more complex, so that at first it looks like a store-bought book. It, too, is filled with her snapshots of the people she met and the places she visited, as well as fragments of text that unfold in a stream-of-consciousness style. The quilted cover features the shapes of Texas, New Mexico, and Arizona, the three states she visited.

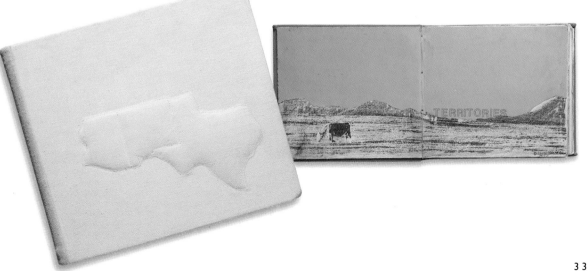

Travel Memories

1.

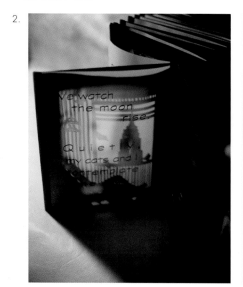

2.

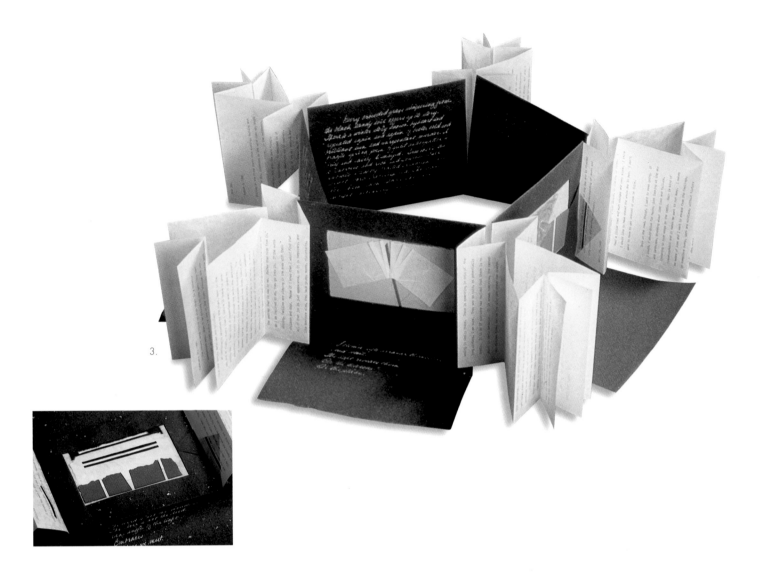

3.

1. FRIENDSHIP, VITALITY, AND STRENGTH

Lonnie Graham

Photogravure images with handset type.
Box: 12" x 11 1/2" x 13 1/2"
(30 cm x 29 cm x 34 cm);
books: 9 5/8" x 7 1/4" (24 cm x 18.5 cm)

Friendship, Vitality, and Strength is the culmination of Graham's pilgrimages to Kenya and other parts of East Africa over a fifteen-year period. It consists of three books—each concertina-bound and covered with handmade tapa cloth imported from East Africa—contained in a box handcrafted from East African wenge and zebra wood.

2. 36 VIEWS OF THE EMPIRE STATE BUILDING

Béatrice Coron

Accordion-fold paper-cutting book.
11" x 9" x 4" (28 cm x 23 cm x 10 cm)

Coron, who has adapted paper-cutting to many different formats, often collaborates with writers. Here, she juxtaposed poems by Marcia Newfield with scenes of the Empire State Building in New York City. The poetry adds to the wistfulness of many of the images. For a picture of a man fishing alone under a bridge, with the iconic building in the distance, the text reads: "Sometimes the fish here are so small, I throw them all back. Sometimes they're just right."

3. MINNESOTA LANDBOOK

Barbara Harman

Tuxedo parchment, Larroque constellation paper and collages made of assorted Japanese papers. 7" (18 cm) pentagram, closed

Harman's book, which folds completely flat and fits into an envelope, contains three texts: a journal about her experiences when she moved to Minnesota; a narrative text about the state's landscape; and a poem about a personal relationship that parallels the other two texts. This is the last in a series of books the artist made about regional landscapes and relationships.

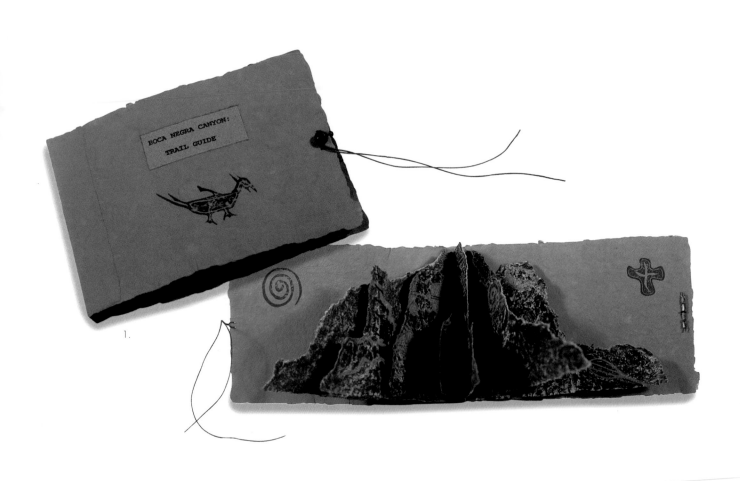

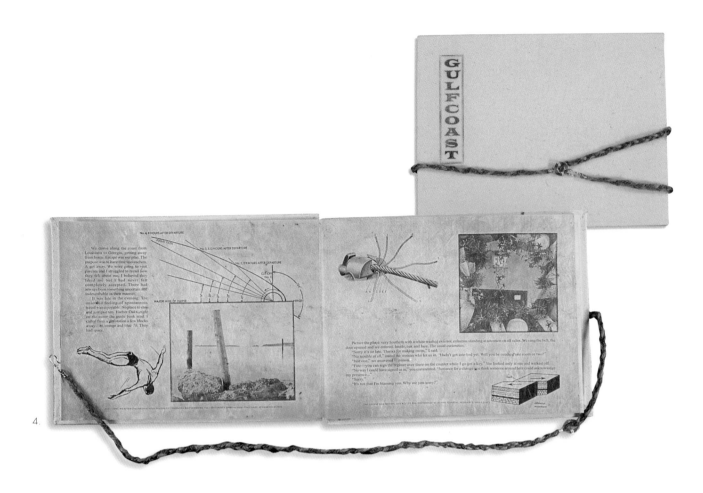

4.

1. BOCA NEGRA CANYON: TRAIL
   GUIDE

   Jody Alexander

   Handbound, with non-adhesive binding,
   and featuring block prints on handmade
   paper. 7" x 5" (18 cm x 13 cm)

   Alexander made four one-of-a-kind
   books as a result of a trip she made to
   New Mexico. In *Boca Negra Canyon:
   Trail Guide,* she wanted to give the
   viewer the feeling of what it was like
   to be among the deep-brown volcanic
   rocks of the canyon, on whose walls
   are etched ancient petroglyphs. She
   also wanted to convey how remarkable
   it is that people are permitted to walk
   freely and unsupervised among these
   treasures.

2. THE COVERED BRIDGES
   OF BUCKS COUNTY, PA

3. THE WINDING ROADS
   OF IRELAND

   Jane Conneen

   Hand-colored drawings on Hahnemuhle
   Bugre paper. 2" x 2 ¼" (5 cm x 5.5 cm)

   Conneen does all her own illustrations, taking photographs during her
   travels and later making pen-and-ink
   drawings for use in her books.

4. GULFCOAST

   David Schlater

   Accordion-fold book of 23 pages; original
   text and photographs/found images; printed
   on Japanese paper using Van Dyke Brown
   photographic process. 8" x 10"
   (20 cm x 25 cm)

   Gulfcoast is based on two very different
   journeys the artist made from New
   Orleans to Alabama. One trip he
   made with a person he was dating,
   and the other was with his mother
   after attending his father's funeral.
   He merged both experiences to relate
   a story of discovery, loss, death,
   and recovery.

1.

2.

3.

1. JOURNEY TALES

Ann Kresge

Seven color-viscosity etchings and letterpress on rag paper, housed in a handmade folio box. 15" x 11" (38 cm x 28 cm)

A travel book in a metaphorical sense, *Journey Tales* consists of etchings Kresge made based on stories and masks by storyteller and sculptor Suzanne Benton. The book visually relates women's stories from the verbal traditions of different cultures around the world.

2. WISH YOU WERE HERE

Emily Martin

Mailing envelopes purchased in England, bound with pencils in a piano-hinge format. 6" x 8" x 6" (15 cm x 20 cm x 15 cm)

The envelopes contain all the postcards—three each day—Martin mailed home while visiting England. The postcards tell the story of her travels, and she included ticket stubs and other related mementos to further describe her experiences. The book is composed entirely of articles collected from her trip—even the pencils used in the binding.

3. THE SHORE

Jill Timm

Accordion-fold book, with color photos, shells, and oat grass. 2 3/8" x 3" (5.5 cm x 8 cm)

Timm's *The Shore* was inspired by a trip she took to the Texas seaside and, appropriately, includes not only her photos (which she scanned and then manipulated in Photoshop) but also oat grass and shells she collected.

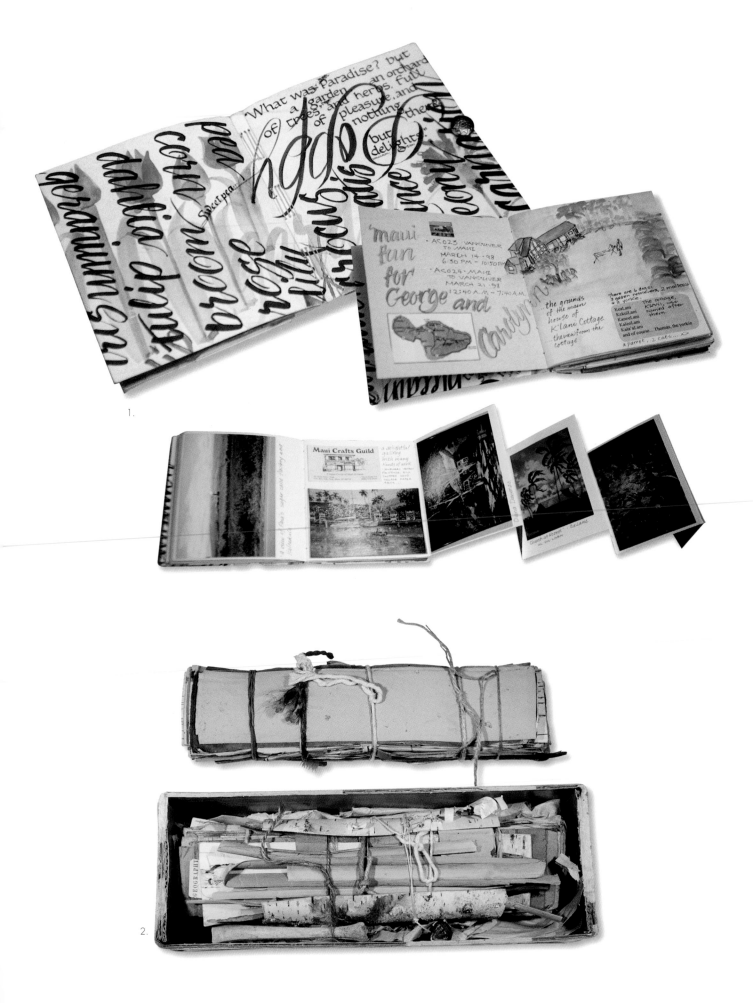

1.

2.

3.

1. MAUI JOURNAL

Carolynn Dallaire

Mixed media. 6 3/8" x 5 3/4"
(17 cm x 14.5 cm)

Dallaire's travel journal shows how
diverse materials can be put to creative
use. *Maui Journal* features not only the
artist's watercolor illustrations and her
husband's vacation photos but also
related postcards, business cards from
their favorite restaurants and galleries,
and clippings from tourist magazines.

2. BACKCOUNTRY TRAVEL PACK

Phil Sultz

Mixed media, including rice and mulberry
paper, birch bark, red rosin. Pack: 12" x 4"
(30 cm x 10 cm); box: 12 1/4" x 4 1/2" (31
cm x 11 cm)

Sultz, who has traveled extensively on
foot and on horseback through the
Rocky Mountains, made this stacked-
page journal for recording notes, collecting samples of vegetation, and
making sketches. It's meant to be
carried in a backpack or saddlebag.

3. BOOK OF FIRE AND LIGHT

Pamela Moore

Copper pages and wood. 8" x 8" x 8" x 1"
(20 cm x 20 cm x 20 cm x 3 cm)

Moore, who years ago left the U.S. to
live in Spain, made this book as an
homage to the desert of Arizona,
where she lived for several years as a
college student. The desert and copper
light there influenced her later work in
copper, she says. The *Book of Fire and
Light* is a celebration of the landscape
that inspired her but that she is no
longer able to visit on a regular basis.
Each of the pages is sanded in a different manner, and the light reflects on
them in a way, the artist says, that
echoes a night campfire, the intense
red of Arizona's skies, and the endless
miles of desert landscape.

1.

2.

3.

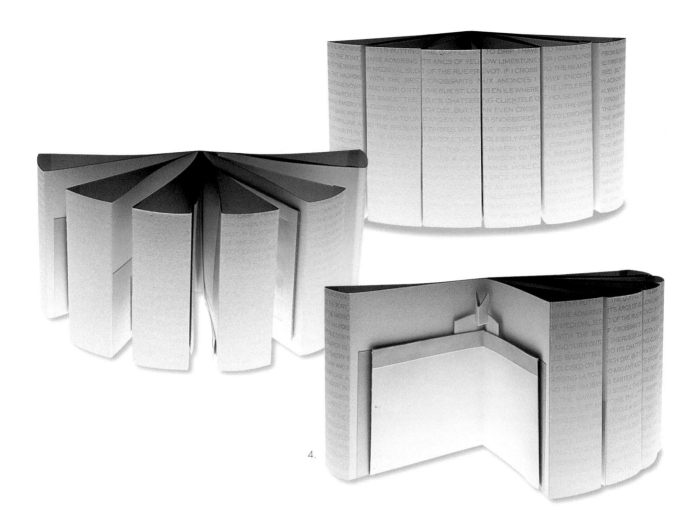

4.

1. SOUVENIR VIGNETTE/YUCATAN

Edna Lazaron

Padded case containing six-page booklet with ceramic covers and consisting of Twin-rocker paper, color copies, and the artist's original photos. 8" x 10" (20 cm x 25 cm)

2. SOUVENIR VIGNETTE/CLASSIC MAYA

Edna Lazaron

Padded case containing four-page booklet featuring artist's own photographs. 6 1/2" x 7 1/2" (17 cm x 19 cm)

Lazaron, an avid traveler, has an ongoing book series she calls "Travel-og Series: Souvenir Vignettes." Her travel books have a scrapbook aesthetic, incorporating sketches she has made on location, fellow travelers' photos as well as her own, and hand-lettered quotations from books related to her trip.

3. ITALIAN PLACES

Evelyn Eller

Mixed media, including wooden box with collaged shelves. 7 1/2" x 5" x 6 1/2" (19 cm x 13 cm x 17 cm)

Inspired by the artist's time as a student in Italy, this book consists of an antique wooden box originally made to store photographs. Eller made shelves for the box and collaged each one with images of a single Italian city and related maps. Each shelf can be pulled out and admired.

4. IN THE MORNING

Mei-Ling Hom

Five wedge-shaped pages with silkscreened pop-up illustrations. 10 3/4" x 6" (27.5 cm x 15 cm)

The text that serves as a decorative pattern on the outside of the book—"Baguettes...croissants"—says it all in this travel book about strolling through the back streets of Paris in search of small neighborhood bakeries.

personal memory books

Technically, all memory books are "personal"—they all relate to the artist's life in one way or another. But for our purposes, personal memory books are about examining the self—the artist getting to know the artist.

Consider the diary. Most people think of diaries as something very predictable: You diligently record the events of your life in it. But life is hardly predictable, so it follows that your journal shouldn't be, either. Don't be afraid to muck it up a little—draw in it, paint in it, make collages in it. Some people even make personal memory books about specific experiences in their life, like moving to a new house.

Personal memory books give artists the ultimate opportunity to indulge themselves, and there's a lot to be learned in the process. Who knows what kind of discoveries you can make along the way?

My House

BASED ON A PROJECT BY SUSAN HENSEL

My *House* started as a written exercise that artist Susan Hensel gave herself to describe her childhood home as if discussing it with a stranger. She then realized there were ways to tie in related writings about her mother. "When you take the time to reflect on certain aspects of your life," she says, "other memories and emotions often well up unexpectedly." So her writing about her home then turned into a book in the shape of a house that looks back on her mother and the rest of her family—even her dog—when she was five years old. Hensel says she remembers the knotty-pine walls of her house in upstate New York, the way the light filtered in through the door, and how the slate floor outside looked when it had been washed down. These are some of the images she evokes in *My House,* which features printed images of a house she encountered as an adult that reminded her of her childhood home.

What You Need

10 sheets black Canson Mi-Teintes paper, 8 ½" x 14" (22 cm x 36 cm)

10 sheets Wausau Royal Fiber, 8 ½" x 14" (22 cm x 36 cm)

Two pieces black mat board, 8 ½" x 7" (22 cm x 18 cm)

One roll heat-activated adhesive

PVA glue

Dry iron

Utility knife

Ruler

Cutting surface

Bone folder

Small, flat brush

Waste paper (such as an old phone book)

step-by-step

1. Making the pages

Cut 10 sheets of Wausau Royal Fiber at 8 1/2" x 14" (22 cm x 36 cm) each to use as the pages. Print, draw on, paint, or otherwise decorate them, keeping the design in the shape of a house. (Hensel printed an image of a house with an image of herself as a child.)

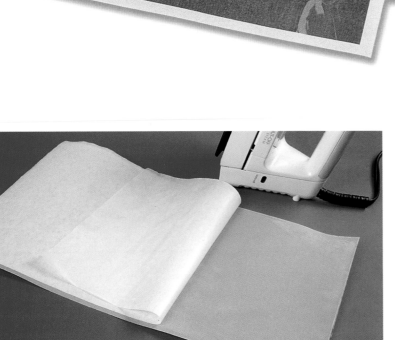

2. Reinforcing the pages (part 1)

Next, cut 10 sheets of black Canson Mi-Teintes paper measuring 8 1/2" x 14" (22 cm x 36 cm). Use this paper as reinforcement for the printed pages and as a decorative element, as the black provides a handsome contrast with the brown pages you've decorated. Then apply heat-activated adhesive to the back of the pages, following the manufacturer's directions.

3. Reinforcing the pages (part 2)

Remove the backing from the adhesive. Using the backing as a pressing cloth, iron the black paper and the pages together.

4. Reinforcing the pages (part 3)

Now trim the excess paper away from the images so that each page is uniformly in the shape of a house, and put aside two pages to use as endpapers.

5. Collating the pages

Use a bone folder or blunt butter knife to score the center line of each of the pages. Then fold the pages in half along the scored line and stack the folded sheets in the order they will appear in the book.

6. Gluing the pages together

First, apply a strip of glue to the back of the right-hand fore edge (the open edge) of the first page. Use waste paper (such as the pages of an old phone book) to prevent excess glue from ruining the other pages. Then carefully place the next page onto this strip of glue and rub it down to make sure it will stick. Repeat this process for all of the pages to create an accordion-fold book.

7. Making the covers

Cut two 8 1/2" x 7" (22 cm x 18 cm) pieces of black mat board to use as the covers. Apply heat-activated adhesive to the endpapers and adhere them to the mat board, once again using the removed backing cloth from the adhesive as a pressing cloth. Trim the covers to the required size.

8. Adhering the covers to the book

Next, apply heat-activated adhesive to the back of the cover boards and iron the first page of the book to the front cover. Repeat this process for the back cover to finish the book.

9. Making a box for the book

Make a box for the book, as a way to store it and easily transport it. Hensel made her box out of Davy board that she decorated with acrylic paint, modeling paste, and crackle medium.

Variation

I LOOKED DOWN THE HALL

8 ½" x 5 ½" (22 cm x 14 cm)

Halls have great metaphorical significance for Hensel. One day in her current home, she walked out of her office and looked down the hall and was overwhelmed by all her remembered experiences. This was the inspiration for *I Looked Down the Hall,* in which, the artist says, "the rug in the hall symbolizes a river of tears, a river of healing, and a river of baptism."

Journal 1

BASED ON A PROJECT BY JOAN DUFF-BOHRER

Artist Joan Duff-Bohrer takes a free-form approach to journal-making. While her book-binding process is fairly defined (she always makes paste paper to decorate the covers and uses the coptic binding method to assemble her books), her method for filling the pages is best described as anything goes. Above all, this artist believes that a journal should be whatever the owner wants to make it, and all worries about keeping the pages pristine should be cast aside.

What You Need

Paste paper

Scissors

Bone folder

Utility knife

Cornstarch

Wax paper

Electric drill

Waxed linen thread

Curved needle

Pliers

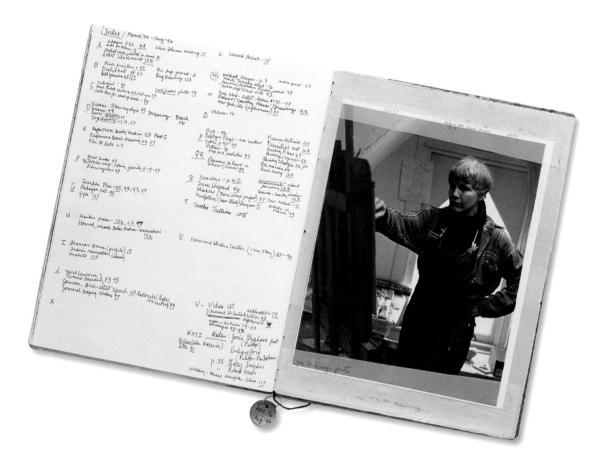

step-by-step

1. Making paste paper for covers

Make paste paper, let it dry, and iron it flat.
Paste paper is made from a mixture of
flour, water, and pigment. It's a great way
to design patterns and colors and is ideal
for Duff-Bohrer's journals, which are
extremely individual.

2. Decorating the covers

Choose a section of the paste paper, using
a frame finder cut from cardboard, for the
covers. (Duff-Bohrer uses cornstarch glue,
which she makes herself, as an adhesive.)
Even her endpaper is handmade: Here
Duff-Bohrer cut endpaper from some of
her old sketches and pasted it onto the
book board. Next weight down the covers,
with wax paper in between them, and let
them sit overnight so they dry flat.

3. Preparing the signatures and spine covers

First fold the signatures (the paper should be
$^1/_2$" [1 cm] smaller in length and height when
folded than the cover size). There are eight signatures of four folded sheets each. Note that
the spines for the first and last signature should
be cut differently, with a full page on the outside of each to be used for a title sheet at the
beginning or for a decorative page at the end.

4. Binding

Using a handmade template, poke holes through the signatures and spines. (Duff-Bohrer recommends making the holes no more than 3" [8 cm] apart.) Drill holes in the covers and then align the entire package and wrap it so it will stay in place when sewing. Duff-Bohrer used the traditional coptic binding method.

5. Filling the pages

Duff-Bohrer's journals also function as personal photo albums. Here, the artist is pictured at her easel.

Variation
JOURNAL 2

12" x 9" (30 cm x 23 cm)

Journals are not just for text. Duff-Bohrer likes to include notes to herself, clippings from magazines, photos, sketches—all manner of scraps and mementos that relate to her life.

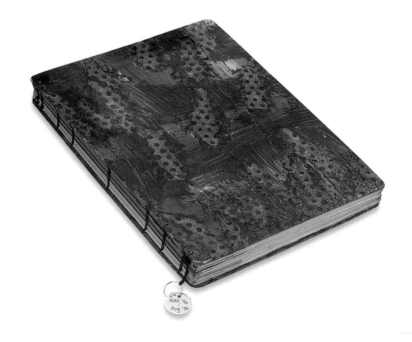

Modus Vivendi

BASED ON A PROJECT BY MARIA PISANO

rtist Maria Pisano was born in Italy, and it remains very dear to her. She says going back is like making a discovery, and she tries to visit a different city each trip. Like many artists who travel to Italy, Pisano comes away from these visits inspired to create art. But because the country holds so much personal significance for her, she is also inspired to reflect on her heritage. In *Modus Vivendi* (Latin for way of living), Pisano explores her past and present and that of her family by way of surrealistic photocollages that combine old family photos and current vacation snapshots. It's an example of how a book's structure can be as significant as what the book contains. *Modus Vivendi* unfolds continuously until you get to its center—representing how memories unfold and unravel, almost as if with their own momentum.

What You Need

Rives BFK paper

Polymer plates

Photographs

Computer with Photoshop

Letterpress

Linen thread

Paste paper

Etching press

Utility knife

Ruler

step-by-step

1. creating images for each page

Pisano's book consists of letterpress prints. To try this, select photos you've taken (Pisano used ones she shot in Italy) along with old family photos, scan them into a computer using a flatbed scanner, and make a photocollage from them using Photoshop. Have a service bureau (a photo-processing store should be able to do it or at least direct you to a service bureau) output the files as negatives to use to make prints.

2. Making plates

Place the negative on a polymer plate (a light-sensitive plate used for printmaking that can be purchased at most art-supply stores) and expose the plate to ultraviolet light. This sets the positive image on the plate. Then rinse the plate to remove the excess polymer, and let it dry. Expose the plate to ultraviolet light a second time to set and harden the polymer, making the plate ready for printing.

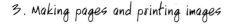

3. Making pages and printing images

To create a book that will fold out continuously, adjust the width of the pages according to their placement in the book. For example, make page one 11" high and 8 1/2" wide (28 cm x 22 cm) and each subsequent page 1/8" (.3 cm) smaller than the previous one. The last page should measure 7 1/2" (19 cm) wide (the height remains constant throughout). Use a letterpress to print your images in black ink.

4. Binding the book

To decorate the cover, Pisano used a collograph plate (a printing plate whose surface has been built and is then incised with the image) and an etching press with silver and black ink. Try using a paste-paper pattern, as Pisano did, to decorate the inside of the cover. To bind the book, cut four paste-paper binding strips of Rives BFK paper to 11" x ³/₄" (28 cm x 2 cm) and fold them down the center. Pair the pages, with the image side facing in, and use 3M series 2-0300 archival double-sided tape to join the paste-paper strips to each pair of pages until all the pages are attached to each other.

5. Finishing the book

Sew the text block to the cover (Pisano used a five-hole pamphlet stitch).

Variation

ECHOES

Case: 8 ¹/₂" x 6" x ³/₄" (22 cm x 15 cm x 2 cm); book: 8" x 6" x ³/₄" (21 cm x 15 cm x 2 cm)

Like *Modus Vivendi*, *Echoes* requires the reader to unravel it, removing the book from its case, and then from a clear plastic cover, to reveal the collection of text (including a letter written by the artist's young son while visiting Pompeii) and family photos.

Personal Memories

1.

1. IT STARTS WITH A TABLEAU

Sandy Groebner

Accordion-fold binding, with hardcovers coated in beeswax, and photographs; housed in a wooden box. 7" x 11" (18 cm x 28 cm) closed

Groebner culled the text for this book from various sources and arranged them in a stream-of-consciousness style for a dreamlike autobiographical narrative.

2. BOOK OF TRANSFORMATION

Donna Marie deCreeft

Mixed media, including Tibetan rice paper, India ink, acrylic paint, collage, linoleum prints, monoprints, and stamp printing. 10 ½" x 11 ½" (27 cm x 29 cm)

DeCreeft calls her books diaries of her unconscious. *The Book of Transformation,* for example, refers symbolically to a year of intense change in her life, using what the artist calls images of potential—seeds, pods, chrysalis, and wings—to suggest her transformation.

3. DREAM LOG

Béatrice Coron

Confetti text paper with photocopied images, 18 pages. 5 ½" x 8 ½" (14 cm x 22 cm)

Coron's dream journal features illustrations she made from paper-cuttings and then photocopied. The pages alternate colors, from yellow, to rust, to tan, with a red cover. Charms hang from extra thread left after sewing the binding.

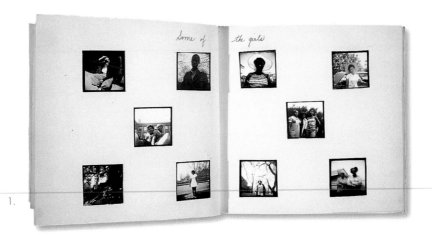

1.

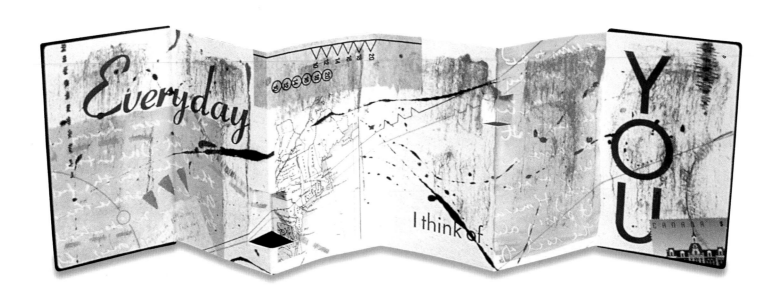

1. UNTITLED
(YOUTH PROJECT BOOK)

Laura Blacklow

Cover with a cotton quilt square, plastic binding, pages of rag paper, original black-and-white photos. 8" x 8" (20 cm x 20 cm)

While a graduate student, Blacklow spent a year working with inner-city teenagers in an art-therapy program sponsored by the National Institutes of Mental Health. This is her journal from that time. It includes photos she took of some of the kids she worked with and befriended. She was not required to do the journal for the program; she says she made it for herself to try to capture what the kids meant to her and what she was learning from them.

2. LETTERS NEVER SENT 1 (JULIA)

Bonnie Stahlecker

Six-panel accordion-fold book; abaca paper with over-beaten pigmented pulp design; letterpress, monoprint, collage, and Prisma-colors. 4 $^7/_8$" x 2 $^3/_4$" (13 cm x 7 cm) closed; 4 $^7/_8$" x 14" x 1 $^1/_2$" (13 cm x 36 cm x 4 cm) when displayed

Stahlecker has made a number of books on the theme of what she calls mind letters—letters she composes in her mind but that will exist tangibly only in the form of a book. Fittingly, these books are somewhat mysterious (she writes text through wet paint and a letterpress label, as if to diffuse it further) and often contain little surprises (this one has reversed pop-ups in the peak folds).

3. THE BOOK OF LETTERS
(DAS BUCH DER BRIEFE)

Laurie Snyder

Color photocopies of collages, 96 pages, hardbound in linen and paste paper. 11" x 8 $^1/_2$" (28 cm x 22 cm)

Snyder made color photocopies of collages she constructed from letters, telegrams, photographs, fabrics, post-cards, stamps and the like. She then inlaid into each collage a vellum page of text, in the style of a letter, that expresses mixed feelings about her German-American, Jewish, and Christian heritage. Most of the correspondence in this book was between her parents, who fled Germany on the brink of World War II.

1.

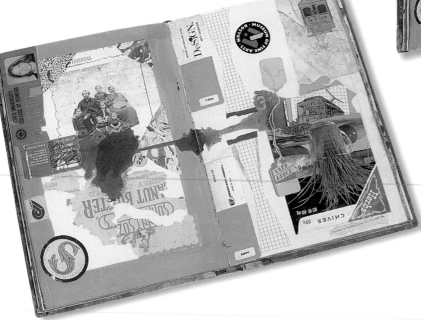

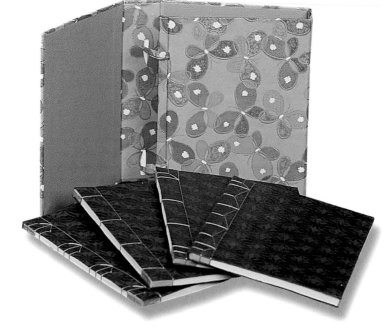

2.

3.

1. AUGUST BOOK AND BOX

Susan Share

Paper, cloth, photographs, acrylic, watercolor, crayon, and collage. 9" x 6" x 1 ¹/₂" (23 cm x 15 cm x 4 cm)

Share created this diary in exactly one month: from August 1 to August 30, 1980. Traveling with a drawing kit consisting of crayons, pencils, paints, colored pencils, glue, and an eraser, she did much of the artwork while on trains and buses en route to visit her uncle, Harvey, who was vacationing in Ogunquit, Maine. Share also collected train and museum admission tickets, labels from food packages and drinks she bought, old family photos, ID cards, and other related materials for her diary.

2. DIARIES WITH WRAPPER

Elizabeth Clark

Four diaries, each with silk-wrapped corners and covered in Japanese paper. 4" x 5 ¹/₄" x ¹/₄" (10 cm x 13.5 cm x .5 cm); wrapper: 4 ¹/₂" x 5 ³/₈" x 1 ³/₈" (11 cm x 13.5 cm x 4 cm)

Clark's diaries chronicle her adventures over the course of a year, with each diary containing the events of a season. The books all have Japanese bindings, but each is sewn a little differently. The wraparound case, called maru chitsu, is designed to hold several volumes.

3. HOMMAGE TO THE WAKING DREAM

Miriam Beerman

Mixed media, collage. 12" x 9 ¹/₂" (30 cm x 24 cm)

Abstract Expressionism was at its height when Beerman started as an artist, and its influence is readily apparent in her work. Her books function as journals, all of them an outlet for self-expression. When she paints and draws in her books, she follows only her intuition as opposed to planning what an image will look like. She says the mark-making process "stimulates and calms me. These marks are the equivalent of words—my language. They are the connecting link between the subconscious and the page."

1.

2.

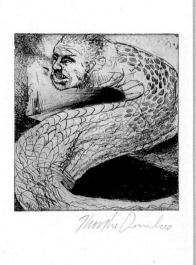

1. JUBAL'S DIARY

Judy & Michael Jacobs

Mixed media. 9 ¼" x 5 ¾" x ⅝"
(23.5 cm x 14.5 cm x 1 cm)

Jubal's Diary is a science-fiction journal meant to be from the future, with sketches of topography and vegetation on a newly discovered planet. Both books feature stub bindings and fit into a hand-painted canvas belt pouch so you can write as you go.

2. HOUSE BOOKS I-IV

Laurie Snyder

Cyanotype vertical accordion-fold books, hardbound in cloth. 85" x 15" (216 cm x 38 cm) open; 14" x 15" (36 cm x 38 cm) closed

Snyder's four hanging books deal with the love of home and the emotions brought on by a move. When folded, the books open like a letter to create a house form.

3. DREAMER DREAMING

Deborah Davidson

Handmade paper of flaxen cotton. 10 pages. 22" x 14" (56 cm x 36 cm)

This is one of several books Davidson made in response to a series of narrative dreams she had about her father, who had died long before. She and her father are the two personae in this book, which includes a poem she wrote that begins: "My father is searching through my dreams, through my psyche for himself. Myself. The dreams are a journey. I am the conduit and the recipient." The back of each of the pages is a solid color that goes from light to dark, alluding to the transition from waking to the dream state.

4. REAL THINGS PEOPLE SAID AND I DIDN'T KNOW WHAT TO SAY

Thorsten Dennerline

Accordion-fold book with nine copper-plate etchings on handmade paper, bound in leather. 7" x 6" x 2" (18 cm x 15 cm x 5 cm)

Dennerline's book, which is meant to be simultaneously critical and humorous, contains a selection of things people really said that left the artist flummoxed.

3.

1. DON'T BUG THE WAITRESS

Susan Baker

Folder with pockets, containing hand-silkscreened images on acid-free paper. 14" x 10" (36 cm x 25 cm)

All of Baker's books are autobiographical. In this book, the artist takes a humorous look at her experiences as a waitress.

2. HOWARDS & HOOVERS: A SAMPLE BOOK OF CHINESE-AMERICAN MALE NAMES

Indigo Som

Letterpress, watercolor, and laser-print fan book. 7" x 2" x 1 ¼" (18 cm x 5 cm x 3.5 cm)

Som uses her books to explore the eccentricities, mundane particulars, and cultures, as she puts it, of her many communities—Asian/Pacific Americans, women of color, and progressive activists, among others. She says she prefers humor and irony to dogma. In this book on Chinese-American first names, she examines community and identity in a very quiet but profound way.

3. LITTLE ORPHAN ANAGRAM

Susan Bee and Charles Bernstein
Mixed media. 11" x 8 ½" (28 cm x 22 cm)

This book, which features collages of original and found images, such as pictures from nineteenth- and early twentieth-century children's books, is a dreamlike interpretation of childhood.

1.

2.

1. DAILY PLANNER

Kez van Oudheusden

Painted silk-covered book with recycled handmade paper and pigskin spine. 7" x 5" x 1" (18 cm x 13 cm x 3 cm)

Most people carry a Filofax as their day planner, but Van Oudheusden has made one of her own design that will be saved as an artwork and a personal archive.

2. PHOTO ALBUM WITH BOX

Elizabeth Clark

Suede-covered photo album with inset of faux leopard fur; album is housed in a cloth-covered clamshell box. Book: 5 1/8" x 5 1/8" x 3/8" (13 cm x 13 cm x 1 cm); box: 6 1/4" x 5 1/4" x 1 1/4" (16 cm x 13.5 cm x 4.5 cm)

Clark created this book to house photographs she took of her friend Sophie. The book's structure is a modified accordion: The spine is a mini-accordion, and Clark attached the pages to the "valleys" of the folds.

3. BEGINNINGS

Kamal Boullata

Two-sided format with linocut. 8 3/4" x 4 1/2" (22.5 cm x 11 cm)

Boullata's book features a love poem in English and Arabic by the Arab poet, Adonis. Boullata, a well-known Palestinian painter, scholar, and researcher, also explores geometric patterning and color in this book. As the pages open, the colors change from cool hues like blue to hot reds, oranges, and yellows. The book's two-sided format lends itself perfectly to the bilingual text.

4. DAY JOURNAL

Phil Sultz

Envelope of honeysuckle vine laced with birch bark, with string-bound notebook of mulberry rice paper. Envelope: 7" x 5" (18 cm x 13 cm); notebook: 6" x 4 1/4" (15 cm x 10.5 cm)

Sultz's journal fits neatly into a rustic envelope, perfect for carrying it along where the day takes him.

Family & Friends

You're entering familiar territory when it comes to memory books about the people in your life. Who hasn't filled an album with photos of the ones they love?

Start your memory book by organizing your photographs by subject. Then, think about what other kinds of items go with this subject. For a book on your grandmother, you could gather things that she used or that represent her, such as playbills from her favorite shows.

Finally, design your book to suit your subject. Cover that book on your grandmother, for instance, with a kind of lace similar to what she might have had at her house.

There's really no way to go wrong with this kind of memory book: The more personal and specific you get, the better the book is.

holding
her body

Why don't you wear
your dress
always?

I ask.

NICE SPOT

Evangeline

Sisters

BASED ON A PROJECT BY SHIREEN HOLMAN

In this book about her daughters, who artist Shireen Holman and her husband adopted from India when the girls were infants, Holman includes their passport covers and pictures, a fabric design from their infant clothes, Indian handmade paper, and scenes from their life growing up in the United States. The artist wanted to represent not just the specifics of their lives, though, but also to describe their relationship with one another. So, the front and back covers show the girls first facing away from each other and then reaching out to each other, symbolic of both sibling rivalry and closeness. Holman made *Sisters* from a reduction linocut print that she then folded into a book, to which she added pop-up sections and photographs. As an alternative to linocut printing, though, try painting a single large sheet of paper; creating an image on a computer, printing it out, and then having a giant color copy made of it; or even making a collage of handmade papers to fold into a book with added photographs.

What You Need

Newsprint

Tracing paper

Ruler

Bone folder

Linoleum

Transfer paper

Relief-printing inks

Baren

Ink knives

Drawing paper for sketches

Printing paper for the book

Pencils

Utility knife

Linoleum cutting tools

Black marker (with an ultra-fine point)

Brayers

Spoon

PVA glue

step-by-step

1. Making a mock-up of the book

Make a mock-up out of newsprint the same size as the final book. The mock-up should show where the folds will be. Fold the book in half, then in eighths. Then reverse fold and cut on top.

a.

b.

c.

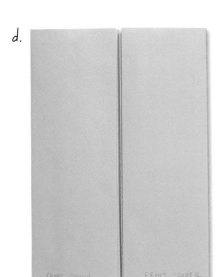

d.

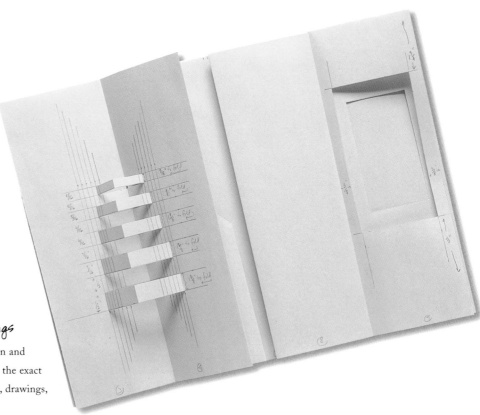

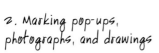

2. Marking pop-ups, photographs, and drawings

Clearly mark the exact location and size of the pop-ups, as well as the exact placement of the photographs, drawings, prints, and other images.

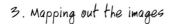

3. Mapping out the images

On tracing paper the size that the final linocut print will be, trace the images in the places they'll need to be in order to appear correctly when the print is folded into a book. Use transfer paper to transfer the drawings to the linoleum block. Go over the lines of the drawing with a permanent marker so it won't be erased after you print the first color. Then cut out the areas of the image to remain white in the final print so that they won't take any ink.

4. Printing the colors

Print the first stage yellow using oil-based relief inks. Roll the ink out onto a glass slab using a brayer. Then roll the ink onto the linoleum block and place the printing paper over the block. Place tracing paper over the printing paper so as not to damage it when transferring the image. Do the actual transfer with a baren and a spoon. Then cut the linoleum block some more, this time removing areas that you want to remain yellow, and print the second color red. Repeat this process, this time printing the final color, dark blue.

5. Folding the paper into a book

When the ink is dry, use a bone folder to crease the folds. Make the cuts necessary for the pop-ups and then paste the photographs in place using PVA glue.

Variation

MEMORIES OF MY FATHER

15" x 11" (38 cm x 28 cm)

Here, Holman made woodcuts and screen prints on handmade paper to once again combine the memories of two cultures. Her father immigrated to the United States from India, where he spent the last thirty years of his life (he died in 1994). *Memories of My Father* is in the form of one large book with several small booklets tucked into pockets. Like *Sisters,* this book also incorporates Indian handmade fabric designs.

Saquish

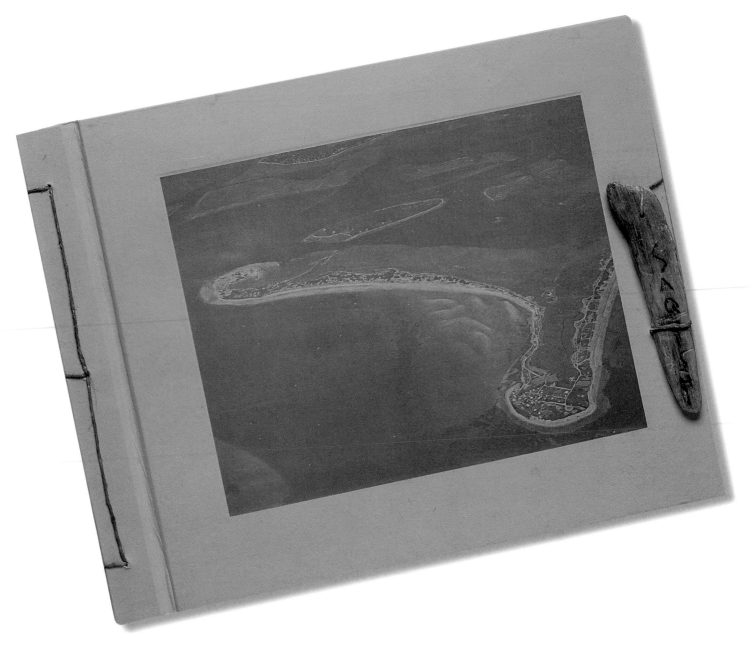

BASED ON A PROJECT BY CATHERINE BADOT-COSTELLO

*G*aquish is a beach community in Plymouth, Massachusetts, where four generations of Catherine Badot-Costello's family have passed enjoyable times at their cottage. Over the years, many members of her family have been inspired by Saquish's marshes, sand dunes, rocky beach, and cozy bay to create art. So the artist decided to create a book of artwork by grandchildren in the family ranging in age from five to sixteen. Their art represents a few of their favorite things about visiting Saquish.

What You Need

Color copies of original artwork and photographs

Driftwood

Archival tape

Acid-free book board

Acid-free paper

PVA glue

Acrylic paint

Bone folder

step-by-step

1. Making the covers

First, cut two 11" x 13" (28 cm x 33 cm) pieces of book board to use as covers. To make a hinge for the book, trim 1 $^1/_2$" (4 cm) from the front cover at the spine edge, and then cut $^1/_2$" (1 cm) from this trimmed piece. Assemble the front cover, gluing the $^1/_2$" (1 cm) piece next to but not flush against the cover board on a strip of book cloth. Badot-Costello recommends gluing a strip of fabric to the front *and* back of the hinge on the front cover to reinforce it.

2. Making the pages

Next, cut pages slightly smaller than the book covers. Then, using the spine of the front cover as a guide, crease each page at the spine edge with a bone folder to provide ease of movement. Tip on (with small points of glue) strips of paper cut to the width of the spine to compensate for the thickness of the pages.

3. Mounting the artwork

Mark the placement of each piece of artwork and attach it to the page with a
hinge made of archival tape. Put two
points of glue at the bottom of the artwork to hold it in place if you don't want
it to flip when the pages are turned.

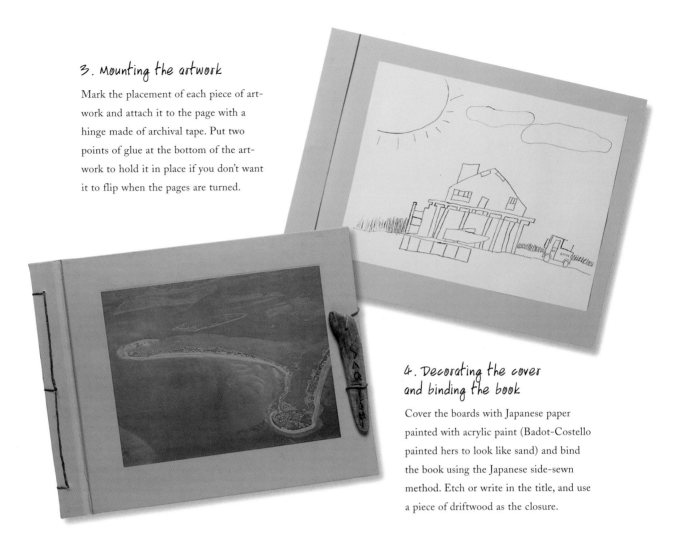

4. Decorating the cover and binding the book

Cover the boards with Japanese paper
painted with acrylic paint (Badot-Costello
painted hers to look like sand) and bind
the book using the Japanese side-sewn
method. Etch or write in the title, and use
a piece of driftwood as the closure.

Variation
LETTERS TO EVANGELINE

8 ½" x 5 ⅝" (22 cm x 14 cm)

To commemorate her grandmother
Evangeline White's ninetieth birthday,
Badot-Costello compiled letters written
by White's five children and thirteen
grandchildren describing their fondest
memories of her. The letters were composed on a computer and laser-printed
on archival paper. Since White was a
gifted seamstress, one of her many quilts
was color copied for the cover of the
book, which was presented to her
grandmother at her birthday party.

Emily & Spot

BASED ON A PROJECT BY RAYMOND H. STARR JR.

*R*aymond H. Starr Jr. was leafing through some snapshots he had taken of his granddaughter, Emily, when he decided that rather than frame the best pictures, he'd use them in a hand-made book. The artist chose seven images that, when arranged in a certain order, told the story of an encounter between a benign-looking but aggressive dog called Spot and a precocious child called Emily. Then he settled on a simple structure for his book: a Japanese stab binding with the boards covered in the same material as Emily's crib sheet. (Getting the material was harder than he expected: It had been discontinued, and he finally had to go straight to the manufacturer for a sheet of it.) The result: a memory book, complete with rubber stamps and photos, that looks at the world through his granddaughter's eyes.

What You Need

Newsprint

Handmade paper

Rubber stamps and ink pads

Book board

Book cloth

Photographs

Paste-paper photo corners

Spray fixative

Acrylic matte medium

Rabbitskin glue

PVA glue

Ruler

step-by-step

1. Making a dummy

Make a dummy for the text block out of newsprint to lay out the pictures and the text. Cut nine pieces of newsprint the size of an unfolded page 6 ¹/₂" x 15" (17 cm x 38 cm), or the size of the available image area. (The actual pages will measure slightly larger, at 6 ¹/₂" x 16 ¹/₂" [17 cm x 42 cm], to allow for the binding.) Then map out the placement of the photos with a cardboard L-shaped template and note the placement of the text and rubber stamps on each page.

2. Making the covers

Cut book board slightly larger than the text block. Each cover will consist of two pieces of book board, one measuring 7 ¹/₂" x 7 ³/₄" (19 cm x 19.5 cm) and another at 7 ¹/₂" x ³/₄" (19 cm x 2 cm). (Use the smaller piece as the spine.) Then cut book cloth into a piece ¹/₂" (1 cm) larger all around than the overall cover, making its dimensions 8 ¹/₂" x 9 ³/₄" (22 cm x 24.5 cm). Coat the larger piece of book board with a 50/50 mixture of PVA glue and methyl cellulose, and place it on the book cloth so that there's a small margin of cloth on three sides of the board. Then coat the smaller piece of book board with the glue mixture and place it approximately ¹/₄" (.5 cm) away from the larger piece of book board to form a hinge. Using a bone folder and additional glue, fold the fabric over the book board, repeating the entire process for the back cover. Decorate the inside of the covers with a paste-paper design.

3. Making the text block

To make lightweight paper more durable, coat it with a layer each of rabbitskin glue, acrylic matte medium, and spray fixative, in that order. Number each page on the spine edge, where it won't be visible when the book is bound, and, using the dummy as a guide, do all the rubber stamping. Finally, mount all of the photos on the appropriate pages using the same PVA-methyl cellulose mixture used on the covers.

4. Binding the book

Because Japanese stab binding does not include a conventional spine, the book will close flat, even with its two-dimensional pages. Or try an alternative binding such as metal posts used for accounting ledgers (available at office-supply stores). To accommodate material pasted onto the pages, simply insert several strips of paper between each page of the book at its spine—they will act as spacers for the pages.

Variation

MS. MANNERS'S GUIDE TO WATERMELON

3 ½" x 5 ½" x ¾" (9 cm x 14 cm x 2 cm)

Here again, Starr has turned snapshots of his granddaughter into a storybook—this time about her unique approach to dining on watermelon.

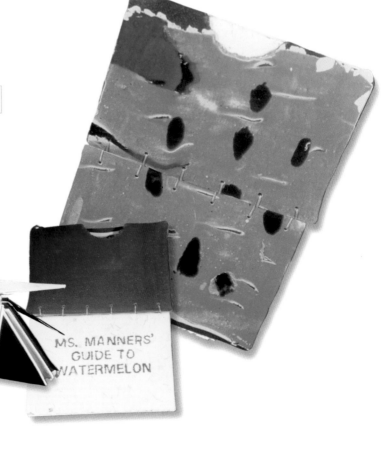

Family & Friends

1.

2.

3.

4.

1. DAYDREAMS FROM A SEASIDE RESPITE

KiP Walker

Mixed media, including cyanotype, beads, thread, Japanese paper. 2 ¼" x 2 ¼" (5 cm x 5 cm)

When she vacations with family at the Carolina shore, Walker likes to bring along an art project to do with her nieces and young cousins. This book, which includes wire, doilies, sand and other found objects, was made from one such visit.

2. MARGARET JANE PASSES ON: A DECLAMATION OF LIFE IN 5 ACTS

KiP Walker

A framed book for hanging, consisting of mixed media, including cyanotype, watercolor, and found objects. 25" x 19" (64 cm x 48 cm)

Walker's book reflects on her mother's life and what she passed on, as well as her death. Her life is described in stages: Child, Lover/Widow, Mother, Teacher, and The Final Passing. The book started with the artist's notion that the common phrase "she passed on" encompasses much more than just a person's death. Her book includes contributions by other family members, as well.

3. THE HANDS THAT HOLD ME

Emily Martin

Variation on coptic binding, with Japanese and English book papers. 8" x 4" x 2" (20 cm x 10 cm x 5 cm)

Martin often makes what she calls collection books. She gathers together a group of people, traces their hands, and uses the tracings in a book. Alternatively, she might make a book of items collected from a certain location in order to maintain a sense of the place. *The Hands That Hold Me* contains tracings of the hands of seventeen members of her family.

4. OLD WIFE'S TALE

Peter Madden

Handmade paper, solvent transfers, mixed-media accordion-fold book. 7" x 12' (18 cm x 366 cm)

This book spans Madden's grandmother's entire life. The text was written by the artist's grandparents, Marie and William Sidley, whose presence is a tangible part of the book. The crocheting at either end of the book was done by Madden's grandmother at the turn of the century, and the beads that hold the book shut were all restrung from her necklaces and earrings.

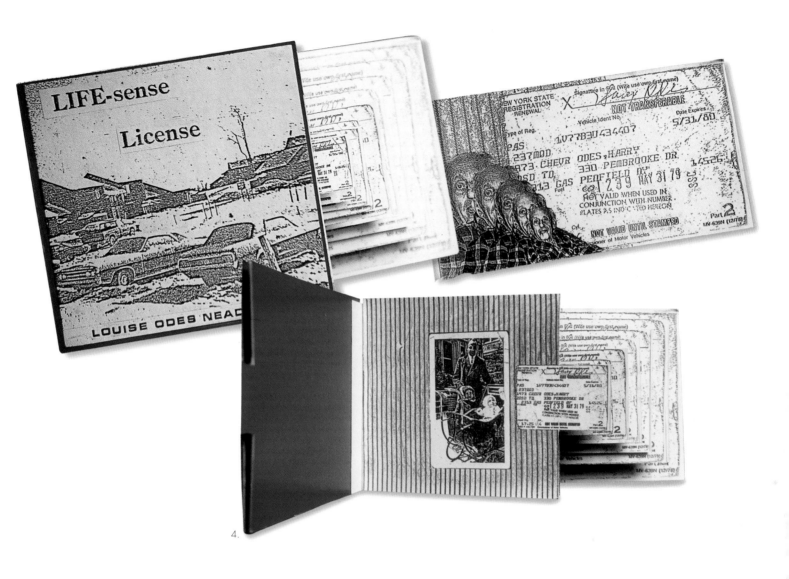

4.

1. LULLABY FOR KENDRA

Susan Kapuscinski Gaylord

Mixed media, including color photocopies, gold marker, colored pencil, and Japanese paper. 10" x 13" (25 cm x 33 cm)

On a visit to the Children's Museum in Boston, the artist and her three-year-old daughter spent a lot of time in a little room where the familiar lullaby, "Mockingbird" ("Hush little baby, don't say a word. Papa's gonna buy you a mockingbird..."), played over and over. There was a display case containing all the objects mentioned in the song. The artist made a book of the song for her daughter, Kendra, changing papa to mama and collecting pictures from catalogs and magazines to represent each of the objects.

2. A PURPLE DRESS

Kerrie Carbary

Accordion-fold stuffed fabric book, with relief prints and photocopies held together with purple ties. 6" x 4 1/2"; folds out to 9' (15 cm x 11 cm; folds out to 274 cm)

Carbary's mother made this dress, a housedress of sorts, when the artist was a child. Carbary says she always wanted a dress just like it, but she and her mom never got around to making it. The artist thinks of this purple dress as a symbol of her mother's spirit and her life.

3. KAPUSCINSKI FAMILY BOOK

Susan Kapuscinski Gaylord

Laser-printed text, black-and-white and color photocopies, photographs, maps, rubber stamps, and gold Chinese spirit paper. 10 1/2" x 8 1/2" (27 cm x 22 cm)

The artist made this book as an example for a project on family history books. It concisely relates the story of her family, starting with her grandparents' arrival in America and ending with the birth of her son.

4. LIFE-SENSE/LICENSE

Louise Neaderland

Twelve board pages, duotone black and brown photocopies. 10 2/3" x 6" x 7/8" (27 cm x 15 cm x 3 cm)

Neaderland's book follows the life of her father, starting when he first got his driver's license, depicting its growing importance to him (particularly when he had a family), and how he refused to give it up even when he was no longer capable of driving a car.

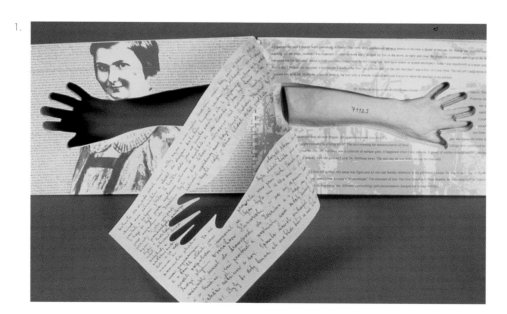

1.

2.

3.

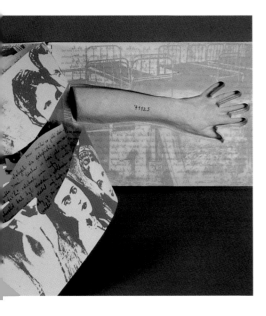

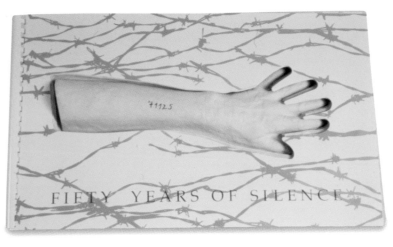

4.

1. 71125: FIFTY YEARS OF SILENCE

Tatana Kellner

Mixed media, including photographs, die-cut pages, and a handmade paper cast, all housed in a wooden box. 12" x 20" x 3" (30 cm x 51 cm x 8 cm)

Kellner's book details her parents' memories of internment in several concentration and extermination camps during World War II. She translated her parents' handwritten Czechoslovakian text into English (the original manuscript is reproduced on transparent interleaved pages). The pages fall around a plaster cast of her mother's arm, which bears the tattooed number she was given in the camps.

2. ALBUM

David Schlater

Computer laser printouts, photographs, and color copies. 12 1/2" x 9 1/2" (32 cm x 24 cm)

The artist got the inspiration to create *Album* when he inherited a stack of deteriorating photos and memento albums, which spanned half a century, from his grandmother. These albums documented her life from when she was a young child, to her dating and high school experiences, to her first marriage, to her husband's death. Schlater, who had never known his grandfather, chose to reproduce some of these materials and make his own album, one that would better stand the test of time—and that presented his new acquaintance with this mysterious member of his family.

3. UNTITLED GIFT BOOK

Mindell Dubansky

Felt pages and linen cover, with cotton embroidery floss, shell buttons, and pearl beads. 6 3/4" x 6" x 1" (17.5 cm x 15 cm x 3 cm)

Dubansky made this book for her mother, who is fond of sewing. The book is based on traditional nineteenth-century needle books made with felt pages that women used to store their collection of sewing needles or pins.

4. FRAGMENTS FROM THE PAST

Evelyn Eller

Mixed media, including color photocopies, monoprints, collage, and Oriental papers. 10 1/6" x 12 1/2" (25 cm x 32 cm)

When this book is standing up, its pages fold out like a sail, making this a sculpture as much as a book. The book visually chronicles Eller's parents' lives when they were young, including their engagement and wedding pictures.

1.

2.

3.

4.

1. MILESTONES

Evelyn Eller

Mixed media, including a cigar box, Indian and Japanese papers, and photocopies. 8" x 8" x 1" (20 cm x 20 cm x 3 cm)

Each page of this book represents a highlight in the artist's life, including her graduation from college, her wedding, and the birth of her children.

2. MARBLE BOX

Elizabeth Clark

Binder's board with Moriki (Japanese paper), bone clasp, hinge whittled from a chopstick, glass-covered opening, and 45 glass marbles. 4 ⁵⁄₈" x 4" x 4 ¹⁄₈" (11 cm x 10 cm x 10 cm)

Each of the forty-five marbles in Clark's treasure box represents a day in the six weeks she spent visiting with a close friend of hers from Thailand.

3. TRANSMUTATION

Lois Polansky

Mixed-media accordion-fold book with hand-made paper. 16 ¹⁄₂" x 62" (42 cm x 157 cm)

Part of a series Polansky did on her family, *Transmutation* is an extremely personal book about the artist's mother, and the technique behind it is very much related to the subject matter. The book features prints by Polansky, except instead of preserving the plate between printings, she changed it each time. After many printings, nearly all the details of the image were removed from the plate except for the silhouette. Not long after she finished this book, her mother became seriously ill, making the fading images of *Transmutation* a haunting suggestion of what was to come.

4. SOME OF MY MOTHER'S THINGS

Laurie Snyder

Eighteen silver prints, dry-mounted on Mohawk paper, one platinum 4 x 5 photograph, hardbound in linen and cyanotype, Florentine endpapers. 14" x 28" (36 cm x 71 cm) open; 14" x 14" (36 cm x 36 cm) closed

Snyder's book documents and celebrates her mother's home (the artist's childhood home). She photographed collections of her mother's things, such as a desk drawer of eyeglasses, boxes of keys, boxes of letters, music stands, her bathrobe, her garden, and so on. The sequence of photographs make what Snyder calls an homage portrait.

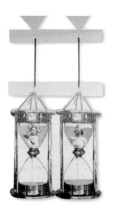
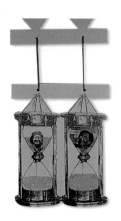

1.

3.

2.

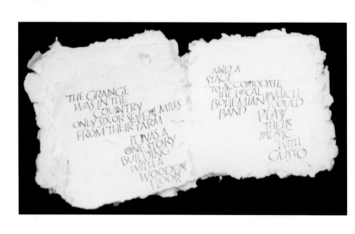

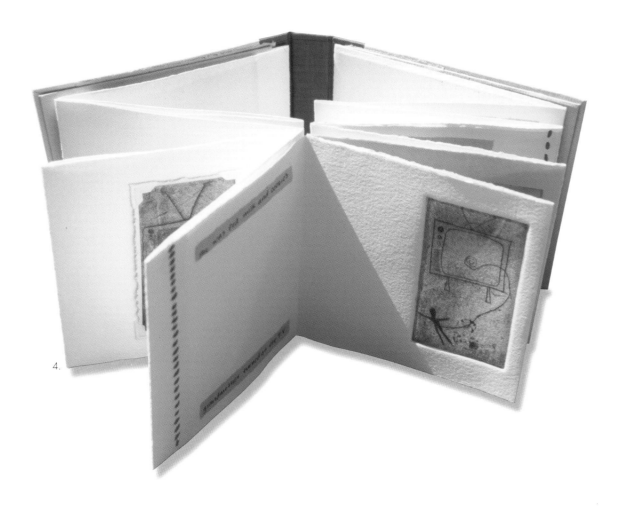

4.

1. OUR GLASS

Louise Neaderland

Seven hand-cut pages with real sand that filters to the bottom of the last page as the pages are turned. 7" x 10" (18 cm x 25 cm)

Here the artist depicts her mother's life, from young girl to old woman, with the sand starting at the top of the hourglass and filtering to the bottom as the pages (which are similar to calendar pages, another reference to time) are turned. This book is part of Neaderland's series, "Where Is Home?," about her parents, the passage of time, and the endurance of sand. The books were made over a period of about four years when both her parents were in nursing homes, a traumatic time for the artist and her sister.

2. 2 SIDES OF A QUILTER

Pamela Paulsrud

Unbound, with calligraphy, letterpress, linoleum block, and cyanotype prints on handmade paper. Cover: 7" x 7 ¹/₂" (18 cm x 19 cm); pages: 5" x 5" (13 cm x 13 cm)

Paulsrud's mother wrote the text for this book about Paulsrud's grandmother, a quilter who also liked to go dancing. The title derives from the artist's desire to show another side of her grandmother. So many books have been written about quilters and quilting, she says, but a quilt has more than one side—and so do those who make them.

3. UNTITLED HANDBOOK WITH PREDICTION

Crystal Cawley

Mixed media, including handmade Japanese paper, acrylics, ink, and rub-on type; with handmade box. 7" x 4" (18 cm x 10 cm)

Cawley, who says she has an obsession with hand shapes, made this book at a time in her life when a friend of hers was fighting a losing battle with a fatal illness. The striking images in this book were influenced by ones she saw on billboards while traveling in Paris and Prague.

4. AT GRANDMOTHER'S HOUSE

Kerrie Carbary

Accordion-fold book, with hand-printed etchings and hand-lettered text. 6" x 6" (15 cm x 15 cm)

Carbary's book features her own text about her relationship with her grandmother, touching on shared heritage, the television as babysitter, and aging.

special events

THE MOMENTS OF YOUR LIFE

Making a memory book about the important events in life is a way to both relive the experience and marvel at all that went into it.

Let's say you were planning a family reunion. You could make a memory book that would include old family photos and new pictures from the reunion. You could even get everyone else to contribute something, whether it be an anecdote or pictures from their own life. When it was done, the book would be a family chronicle.

There are so many times in life that are turning points, and then plenty that are simply notable side roads. In either case, they all go by so fast, and some of them we would like to revisit at our own pace. Memory books make that possible.

Mini Wedding Book

BASED ON A PROJECT BY STEPHANIE LATER

Artist Stephanie Later started making wedding books as gifts; they were an engaging means of encompassing everything that leads up to a wedding—from cards and telegrams to party favors from the shower and engagement party. She is especially fond of the accordion-fold wedding book because it can be filled with favorite photographs and mementos, and displayed at home, as you would a framed picture. Plus, it's easy to take with you on those visits to family members who may have missed the big event.

What You Need

Book cloth

Decorative lace, embroidered items (linens from flea markets, old clothing, etc.)

PVA glue

Bone folder

Ruler

Utility knife

Cutting surface

Archival binder's board

step-by-step

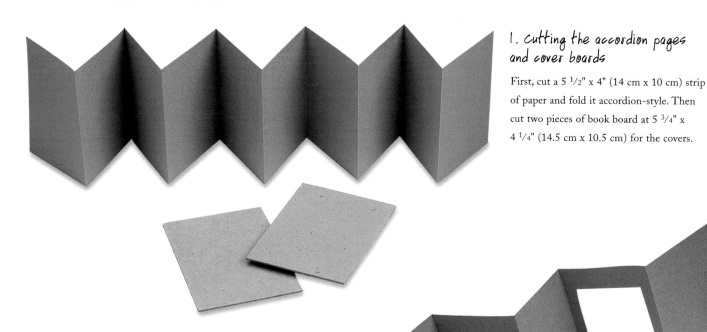

1. Cutting the accordion pages and cover boards

First, cut a 5 $\frac{1}{2}$" x 4" (14 cm x 10 cm) strip of paper and fold it accordion-style. Then cut two pieces of book board at 5 $\frac{3}{4}$" x 4 $\frac{1}{4}$" (14.5 cm x 10.5 cm) for the covers.

2. Placing the photos

To give the effect of framing the pictures, make cutouts in some of the pages as an alternative way to display the photos. Vary the dimensions of the cutouts for added interest. Leave the first and last pages whole to serve as endpapers.

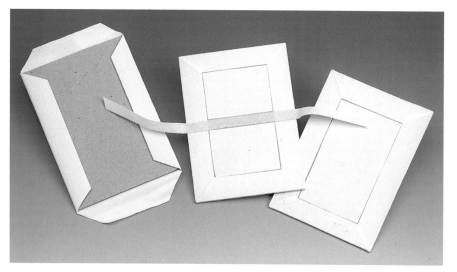

3. Making the covers

Glue the cover boards onto the fabric and trim the edges. Then glue a piece of ribbon across the inside center of the bottom cover to serve as the closure for the book. Cover the exposed book board with extra fabric.

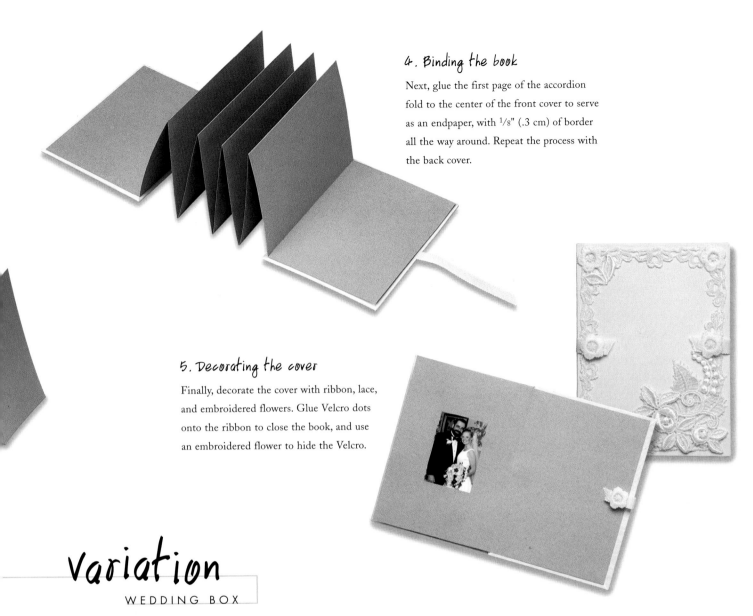

4. Binding the book

Next, glue the first page of the accordion fold to the center of the front cover to serve as an endpaper, with $1/8$" (.3 cm) of border all the way around. Repeat the process with the back cover.

5. Decorating the cover

Finally, decorate the cover with ribbon, lace, and embroidered flowers. Glue Velcro dots onto the ribbon to close the book, and use an embroidered flower to hide the Velcro.

Variation
WEDDING BOX

13 ¾" x 9 ¾" (35 cm x 24.5 cm)

Later created this wedding box to house keepsakes such as the wedding garter, dried flowers, and a piece of the bride's veil. (Later, who has worked as a conservator at the Metropolitan Museum of Art in New York City, emphasizes the importance of using archival materials for boxes and books so they will stand the test of time.) She lined the box with beautiful handmade paper with flowers pressed into it. Or, to make it more personal, she'll write a love poem around the border in gold pen.

Wedding Photo Album

BASED ON A PROJECT BY RAVEN REGAN

*R*aven Regan enjoys making this style of book because it can be customized for any purpose. It measures 9" x 11 ¹/₄" (23 cm x 28.5 cm), so standard 8 ¹/₂" x 11" (22 cm x 28 cm) paper fits perfectly inside. The weight of the pages can vary from a quality bond for a guest book, to a card stock for a photo album, to handmade paper for a gardener's journal. The covers are equally versatile, with papers, ribbons, or patterns used as decoration. Regan personalizes her wedding books by using colors and ribbons she knows the bride likes and by including an invitation to the wedding on the cover—and perhaps even using a quotation of significance to the couple.

step-by-step

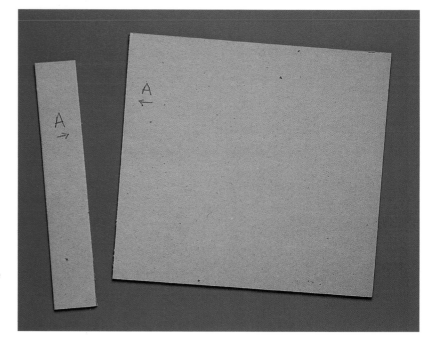

1. Cutting the covers

Cut two pieces of Mill board to 9" x 11" (23 cm, x 28 cm), and then cut a 9" x 1 1/2" (23 cm x 4 cm) strip from each of these cover boards. Use the smaller strips for the spine.

2. Covering the boards

Thin some PVA glue with water, making it the consistency of coffee cream. Then use a 1" (3 cm) sponge brush to apply the glue to the back of each cover board and adhere them to the inside of the decorative paper. Make the boards flush on the binding side (the left side) and centered, with equal margins of paper on the other three sides. Then fold the cloth over and turn the two corners in at a 45-degree angle; glue the paper to the board. Finally, glue the endpapers to each board.

3. Adding binding cloth to covers

To create the hinge of the book, lay out an 11" x 5" (28 cm x 13 cm) piece of book-binding cloth and position the cover and spine on it about $^1/_4$" (.5 cm) apart. Glue the boards to the cloth, and fold the cloth over to completely encase the spine and the edge of the cover. Repeat this process for the back cover.

4. Making the pages

To make the pages fold back easily, score each one 1 $^3/_4$" (4.5 cm) in from the left at the spine with a bone folder. If necessary, add spacers at the spine measuring 8 $^1/_2$" x 1 $^1/_2$" (22 cm x 4 cm) cut from the same paper as the pages.

5. Binding the book

To use a Japanese side-sewn binding, as Regan did here, mark and drill five holes along the spine (through the cover boards, pages, and spacers, which you should clamp together to keep them from moving). Make the end holes 1" (3 cm) in from the top and bottom (or head and tail) of the book. The other holes should be 1 3/4" (4.5 cm) apart. Indent all the holes 3/4" (2 cm) from the binding edge, then sew the book together with ribbon.

6. Decorating the cover and pages

Embellish the decorative-paper cover with cut-out hearts, ribbon, gold photo corners, and charms. For the inside, add photos with gold photo corners and text written in gold marker.

Variation

MATRIMONY MOMENTS

9" x 11 ¼" (23 cm x 28.5 cm)

To make a different book using the same structure and binding, add a framed wedding photo to the cover and embellish it with braided ribbon and a heart locket.

Home Design Folio

BASED ON A PROJECT BY DEBORAH WAIMON

aimon's *Home Renovation Folio* can serve two functions. You can take it with you as you make the rounds to paint stores, furniture showrooms, antique shops, and anywhere else your renovation plans may take you. Use it to collect business cards, paint chips, and fabric swatches. Or, you can use the book as a means of documenting the actual renovation of the house, filling it with photos of the house in progress. For this artist, the practicality of this folio structure is exactly what makes it appealing.

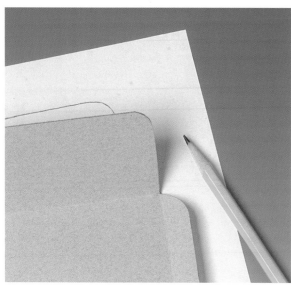

1. Making the envelopes

Make an envelope pattern by opening an existing envelope and using it as a template. The envelope used here is 4" (10 cm) wide and 5" (13 cm) long, but any size can be used. Trace the pattern onto the paper you have chosen, then cut out five envelopes, score along the fold lines, and fold into shape (do not glue together yet!).

2. Making the spine

To make the accordion spine, cut a piece of paper $1/4$" (.5 cm) wider than the folded envelope—here 4" (10 cm)—and twice the length of the envelope—here 14 $1/2$" (37 cm)—plus 4 $1/2$" (11 cm). To create folds in the accordion spine, measure 5 $1/8$" (13 cm) down from the top—this is the length of the folded envelope plus $1/8$" (.3 cm)—make a score line and make the first fold. Continue scoring and folding at $1/2$" (1 cm) increments until there are nine folds and five "valley" folds.

3. Adding the envelopes to the spine

Next, put a scored and folded (but unglued) envelope into the valley of the spine and clip it with clothespins. Measure $3/4$" (2 cm) in from each side of the spine as shown; make a row of seven equally spaced pencil marks in the valley, then poke each mark gently through with a needle. Repeat with all the valley folds.

4. Attaching the envelopes

To begin sewing, cut an 8" (20 cm) length of thread (this is twice the width of the envelope) and sew the bottom of the envelope to the spine, as shown. Leave a 3" (8 cm) "tail" of thread. Sew all six stitches across and back, meeting up with the tail. Tie the ends together with a double knot and dot it with glue.

After each envelope has been stitched, glue the seams together (but don't glue the opening!).

5. Binding, (part 1)

Cut two pieces of narrow ribbon approximately 5" (13 cm) long. Turn the folio upside down and slip the end of the ribbon through the first stitch of each "mountain fold." Repeat this process with the second piece of ribbon on the last row of stitches. (If the ribbon begins to fray, try adding a small piece of tape to the end till you are finished.)

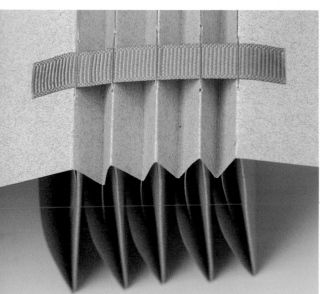

6. Binding, (part 2)

Adjust the tension of the accordion folds—you can pull them tightly together or leave the arrangement very loose, depending on how many items you plan to store in each envelope. Glue the ribbon tabs to the outside of the spine (here each tab is about 1/2" [1 cm] of ribbon).

7. Making the covers

Cut two pieces of book board 4 1/2" (11 cm) wide and 5 1/4" (13.5 cm) long. (This is 1/2" [1 cm] wider than the width of an envelope and 1/4" [.5 cm] longer.) Cover the book boards with book cloth (decorative paper can also be used), and decorate the cover with a collage related to the project. Glue the wider ribbon underneath the collage to use as a tie closure for the folio.

Glue the accordion folio to the uncovered sides of the book board, being careful to center it. Weight down the covers with a heavy object while the glue dries.

Variation

GARDEN FOLIO

5 ½" x 4 ½" (14 cm x 11 cm)

Waimon's envelope folios are endlessly adaptable. Here she used the format to create a garden book for keeping seed packets, before-and-after photos, and notes regarding the planning and planting of a garden. The book can also be used to store dried flowers. Waimon's collaged cover incorporates actual leaves and pictures of flowers in lieu of a title to suggest the contents.

Making Memory Boxes

the basics

All of the box projects in this book refer to the techniques and processes described here. There is a comforting repetitive quality to the steps involved in boxmaking. In the beginning you will refer to these pages often. Soon, you will not even need to peek at them.

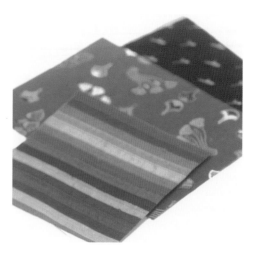

THE PARTS OF THE BOX

A box is composed of several separate units: The case, the flaps, the tray, and the lid. The case, consisting of a front, spine, and back, is constructed by assembling the boards on the covering material, often leaving a space between the boards (called a joint) to act as a hinge.

The most basic box is a simple case with no flaps, no trays, and no lid.

Flaps are panels attached to the case at the top (head), bottom (tail), and side (fore edge). They can be made separately and glued onto the case, or they can grow from the case itself. Flaps keep the contents of the box from falling out.

Trays consist of base boards with walls glued to them prior to covering. Trays are three-walled or four-walled, depending on the style of box.

Lids, either freestanding or attached to the spine, are panels built to extend slightly beyond the parameters of a tray. They create a lip for easy accessibility and lifting and are often embellished with knobs, buttons, ribbons, and other fasteners.

GRAIN DIRECTION

Anyone who has ever torn an article out of a newspaper has had a lesson in grain direction: Pulled in one direction, the paper tears beautifully. But when pulled in the perpendicular direction, the paper rips jaggedly. The clean tear is with the grain; the ragged one, against the grain.

Grain is inherent in paper, cloth, and board. It is determined by an alignment of fibers. The direction in which most of the fibers are aligned is the grain direction of the material.

WHY GRAIN MATTERS

For the moveable parts of a box to work easily and without stress, the grain must run parallel to this hinging action. In a book, grain runs parallel to its spine, making it easy to turn the pages and manipulate the cover. The same is true in boxmaking. The grain must run parallel to the spine of the box.

Understanding grain direction is also important for predicting the stretch of materials as they come in contact with moisture (adhesives). Materials expand opposite their grain direction. If a piece of lining paper is cut to fit perfectly within a box, after pasting it will have stretched in width (against

its grain) while having remained unchanged in height (with the grain). It is necessary to anticipate this stretch and to trim paper accordingly before pasting or gluing.

how to determine grain

The best way to determine grain is through your sense of touch.

For paper and cloth, gently bend (don't crease!) the material and roll it back and forth several times. Let the paper or cloth relax, then bend and roll it in the opposite direction. The direction in which you feel the least resistance is the grain direction.

For board, hold a corner in both hands and flex it, then release the board. Flex the board in the opposite direction. The flexing direction of least resistance is the grain direction.

the basics: *measuring and cutting*

CUTTING

In addition to the hand tools described earlier, a wonderful piece of equipment is a paper cutter. Whether tabletop or freestanding, a paper cutter (or the more substantial board shears) makes the difference between easy and laborious cutting. A good cutter that has a bed with a true edge perpendicular to the cutting edge, a clamp to hold the material in place, and a pair of sharp upper and lower knives is a joy to use. If a cutter is not available, use a utility knife and a T-square.

To ensure accuracy in cutting, you must follow a four-step process.

1. Determine grain direction of the board. (Review Grain Direction on page 116 if you need help with this.) Grain direction must run from head to tail on all boards.

2. Rough cut the board to the approximate size needed for the box. An oversized board is difficult to handle and will not fit on a tabletop paper cutter.

3. Square the board by trimming one long edge of board and a perpendicular short edge to form a true right angle.

4. Mark the board by placing the object to be boxed on the squared corner and making penciled markings of desired height and width.

To determine the depth of the object to be boxed, crease a scrap of paper to form a right angle; slide this scrap under the object and make a parallel crease in the scrap paper, snugly enclosing the object within these two creases. Transfer this measurement—the distance from one crease to the other—to your board.

MEASURING

All boxes start from the inside out. The first piece of board to be measured and cut is the base board, the piece on which your objects (books, photos, marbles) will sit. All of the other boards take their measurements from the base. The base has two dimensions: Height and width.

Height is the distance from top to bottom or, in the bookbinder's language (used throughout this book), from head to tail. Width is the distance from side to side or, more precisely, from spine to fore-edge. The third dimension of the box, its depth, is found in its walls. Depth refers to the thickness of the object to be boxed; the distance, for example, from the top card to the bottom card in a deck of cards.

My approach to measuring is more intuitive than mathematical; I rarely rely on numbers. I love my rulers for their straight edges, not for their numbered markings. Precision is achieved by paying attention to the relationships between the materials and the parts of the box. This book provides you with models to be altered for future projects. When you understand the relationships between the parts and the whole, you will be able to change my patterns and create entirely new boxes.

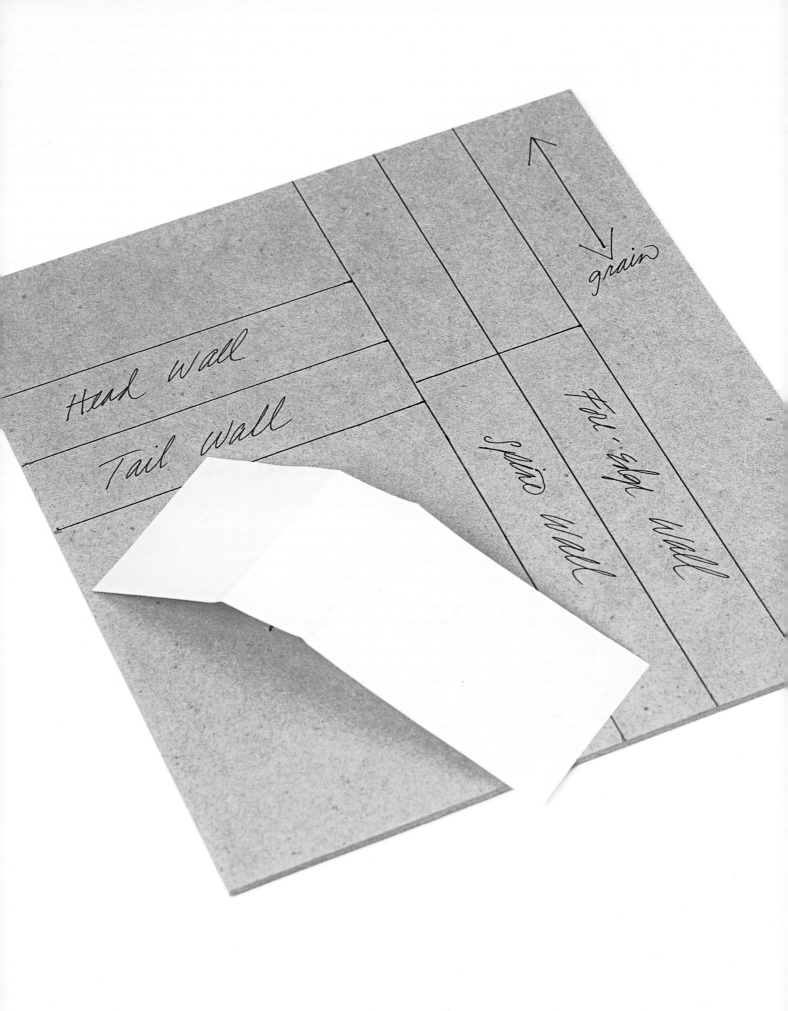

the basics: *pasting and gluing*

PASTING AND GLUING

Pasting refers to the use of any starch-based adhesive. Gluing refers to the use of both full-strength PVA and the more commonly applied mixture of PVA and methyl cellulose.

PAPER   Some papers demand paste; others are happier with the PVA/methyl cellulose mixture. In general, lightweight papers that tend to stretch and curl excessively prefer paste. The high water content in paste saturates the paper and makes it lie down and behave. Similarly, thin, long-fibered translucent papers—like many Japanese tissues—respond better to paste than to mixture. Use mixture on heavyweight papers, which are unlikely to curl and stretch.

CLOTH AND BOARDS   On cloth and boards, always use the PVA/methyl cellulose mixture. The only question is how much PVA? How much methyl cellulose? The answer is determined by the size of your box, the nature of your materials, and the consistency of both adhesives. Remember, a larger box requires more working time (i.e., more moisture) than a smaller box. I usually start with a combination of approximately 70% PVA and 30% methyl cellulose. If my brush drags rather than glides across the surface being glued, my adhesive is too dry. I stop brushing and add another dollop of methyl cellulose to the mixture.

HOW TO PASTE A SHEET OF PAPER TO BOARD

When covering a board with paper, the adhesive must be applied to the paper rather than to the board. If dry paper is pressed onto a wet board, the paper will wrinkle. To paste, place a few layers of newsprint on the workbench. The newsprint should be larger than the paper being pasted. Position your paper face down on the newsprint. Scoop up a generous amount of paste with your paste brush and apply it to the paper with a circular motion, starting at the center of the piece of paper and working outward in concentric circles. Be sure one hand anchors the paper firmly to the newsprint. Keep a paper towel nearby, as you will get paste on your fingers. As you approach the edges of the paper, stop making circles. Return to the center of the paper and brush outward, in radiating strokes, creating a sunburst pattern. Never hold the brush parallel with the edges of the paper: Bristles can slip underneath and stain the surface of the paper. Give the pasted sheet of paper plenty of time to relax before picking it up. If the paper is curling excessively, continue to work your brush across the surface, pressing and flattening. When the paper has been sufficiently saturated with moisture, it will lie flat. Pick up the paper and apply it to the board.

HOW TO GLUE CLOTH TO BOARD

Unlike adhering paper to board, the adhesive can be applied to either the board or the cloth. To glue, follow all procedures as described above, substituting your glue brush for the paste brush and adjusting the PVA/methyl cellulose mixture to suit your materials.

the basics: *making the tray*

HOW TO CONSTRUCT THE TRAY

C-clamp a wooden board onto your tabletop. Set down a piece of wax paper. Place the base board on the wax paper. Using full-strength PVA and a small brush, paint a thin line of glue along the edge of the head wall where it touches the base. Position this wall against the clamped wooden board and push the base against it. (The clamped board supports the wall and helps to maintain a right angle.) Wipe away excess glue with your bone folder. Glue the fore-edge wall, painting the glue along the edge touching the base and also along the edge that meets the head wall. Glue the tail wall, painting the glue along the edge touching the base and also along the edge that meets the fore-edge wall. Glue the spine wall, painting the glue along the edge touching the base and also along the two edges that meet the head and tail walls. Let the tray set until it is dry (15 minutes). Peel the tray off the wax paper, and sand any rough joints. The tray is now ready for covering.

HOW TO COVER THE TRAY WITH PAPER

COVERING THE OUTSIDE

Cut a piece of paper long enough to wrap around all walls, plus 1/2" (1 cm). (If your decorative paper is not long enough, use two shorter pieces; plan the seam to fall at a corner.) In width, the paper should be twice the depth of the tray, plus 11/2" (4 cm).

Paste out the paper. Give the paper time to relax and uncurl. Position your tray, with the bottom of the tray facing you, approximately 3/4" (2 cm) away from the long edge of the paper and 1/2" (1 cm) away from the short edge. Crease the 1/2" (1 cm) extension around the corner and onto the wall.

Roll the tray on the paper, pushing the tray snugly into each right angle as it is formed. Before making the final roll, check the paper for stretch. If the paper has stretched beyond the board edge, trim it to fit. Remember, wet paper tends to tear. To minimize this risk, place a piece of wax paper on top

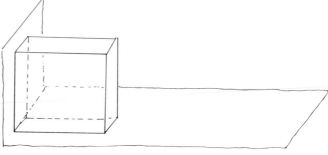

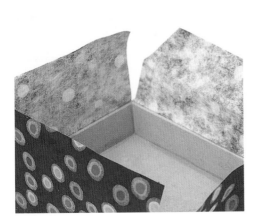  

of the paper to be trimmed, and cut through the wax paper, using a sawing motion with your knife. Use your bone folder to crease the 3/4" (2 cm) turn-ins onto the bottom of the tray. Clip the corners with scissors, and press the paper into position. You are now ready to finish the inside of the tray.

FINISHING THE INSIDE (ABOVE LEFT)   To finish the inside of the tray, slivers of paper exactly one board thickness in width must be removed at each of the four corners. Position the tray on its spine wall, on a cutting mat. Place your metal triangle on the paper. One edge of the triangle should touch the board edge (thickness) while the triangle is slid firmly into the curve of the wrapped paper in the left-hand corner. With your knife, cut through the paper. Start the cut with the tip of the knife actually touching the board. Make a parallel cut, one board thickness away from the original cut. Important: Do not start this cut at the board. With the triangle repositioned, place the knife 11/2 board thicknesses away from the board, and cut. With your knife, make a diagonal cut between the starting points of these two parallel cuts. This cut releases the sliver of paper—one board thickness in width—which allows the covering paper to be turned neatly into the inside of the tray. It also creates a mitered corner. Keeping the tray resting on its spine wall, repeat these cuts in the right-hand corner.

Turn the tray onto its fore-edge wall. Make the cuts, as described previously, in first the left and then the right-hand corners. Note: These cuts are made in only two of the tray's four walls. I have selected the opposite spine and fore-edge walls; you could pick the other pair of opposites, the head and tail walls. Your final cuts are made with scissors. Push the spine wall covering into the tray, pressing it against the inside wall and forcing the paper into the right-angle where the base meets the spine wall. Gently crease the paper by running your bone folder along this seam. Pull the paper back to the outside and cut away the two corners, removing 45-degree triangles of paper. Make sure the cuts stop at the crease mark made in the previous step. Repeat with the fore-edge wall.

(*above middle*) You are now ready to paste. Starting with the head, paste out the covering paper and push it to the inside, pressing it sharply into all seams. Rub with your bone folder to eliminate air bubbles and paste lumps. Repeat at the tail. (Since these two wall coverings have not had slivers of paper removed from them, they overlap the corners. This ensures that the cardboard seam will be covered.) Paste out the spine wall covering and press into place. Paste out the fore edge wall covering and press into place (*above right*).

the basics: *corners and finishing edges*

HOW TO COVER THE TRAY WITH CLOTH

When covering a small tray in cloth, I follow the same procedure described above, substituting mixture for paste.
When covering a large tray in cloth, I prefer to glue out the
boards—one wall at a time—rather than the cloth, and to
work a bit more slowly. Take care to press down the fabric
well as you roll the tray on the cloth. Wrinkles in the cloth
are more likely to develop if the cloth has not been saturated
with the adhesive.

COVERING BOARDS: CUTTING CORNERS AND FINISHING EDGES

Cover papers and cloths are cut to extend 3/4" (2 cm)
beyond the edges of the board to be covered. This extension
is called the "turn-in." Before the covering material is turned
in, its corners must be cut. Both the angle of the cut and its
distance from the tip of the board are crucial.

Apply adhesive to the covering material and press the
board into position. Trim the corners at a 45-degree angle.
The distance between the tip of the board and this cut
should measure 11/2 times the thickness of the board. If you
cut too closely, the tip of the board is exposed. If you cut too
far away, the corner is klutzy. After cutting all corners, re-
apply adhesive to the turn-ins if necessary. Starting with the
head and tail, bring the turn-ins onto the board. First, using
your bone folder, crease the material against the board edge.
Second, flatten the material onto the board, pressing out any
air pockets or bubbles. Use your thumbnail to pinch in the
small sharp triangles of material at the corners. Press firmly so
that the material hugs the corner and molds itself around the
board tip. Now bring the spine and fore-edge turn-ins onto
the board. With your folder, gently tap all corners, eliminating any sharp points or loose threads.

ALTERNATE CORNER COVERING FOR FRAGILE PAPERS

When wet, fragile or thin papers tend to tear. A universal or library corner involves no cutting and is recommended. This treatment is inappropriate for heavyweight papers or cloth; the resulting corner would be too bulky. After pasting the paper and centering the board on it, fold one corner triangle onto the board. Using your bone folder, shape the paper against the board thickness on both top (head) and side (fore-edge). Firmly press the remaining bits (right side of paper) onto the turn-ins below. Repeat at the other corners. With your finger, dab a dot of paste onto the turn-ins, near the corners. Complete the turn-ins (as in above directions). This corner covering yields a gentle, slightly rounded corner.

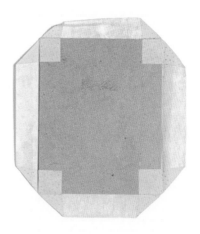

Some photographs, such as these four of a sweet boy named Nicholas, are meant to be displayed rather than hidden away in albums. The Picture Frame Box is a wonderful way to celebrate a specific event—a birth, a graduation, a marriage. A cross between a book and a box, this extended case unfolds, accordion-style, to reveal the four photographs framed within. Make the interior as decorative as possible, and freely mix other mementos, such as birth announcements or fragments of letters, in with the photographs. My preferred covering material is a specific Japanese paper called Momi, *which has the strength and the folding qualities of cloth.*

picture frame box...
memories of a special child

MATERIALS

Two-ply museum board, for mats

Binder's board, for case

Momi paper

Decorative papers (mats)

Decorative papers (linings)

Two bone clasps (also called *tsume*)

Grosgrain ribbon

Mylar

Glue, mixture and paste

getting started: cutting the boards and windows

- Cut the museum board to make four mats. Cut board to desired height and width. Make sure grain runs parallel with the spine edge.
- Cut out the windows in the mats. The windows should be approximately ¹/₂" (1 cm) smaller in both height and width than the photos.

ABOUT MOMI PAPERS These papers are tough enough to be substituted for fabric, but they require special handling. The beauty of these color-saturated papers is in their crinkly surface. If the paper becomes too relaxed—for example, by the application of paste—the crinkles flatten out and the wonderful texture is lost. The solution to this problem is threefold: (1) use mixture instead of paste; (2) apply the mixture to the board rather than to the paper; and (3) don't be too aggressive with your bone folder.

1

2a

2b

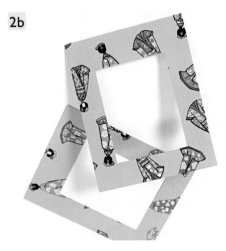

1 Cover the mats. Cut four pieces of decorative paper:

Height = height of mat plus 1¹/₂" (4 cm)
Width = width of mat plus 1¹/₂" (4 cm)

2a PASTE OUT THE PAPER. Center the mat on the paper and press into place. Cut the corners and finish the edges. (see The Basics, page 124). To finish the interior of the mat, make two diagonal cuts, from corner to corner, through the paper in the windows. Remember that wet paper tends to tear when being cut. If your paper is saturated with paste, give it a few minutes to dry before cutting.

2b Prior to pasting these flaps into position on the back of the mats, trim away excess paper with your scissors. Paste. Place the covered mats between sheets of newsprint, and under a board and a weight until dry.

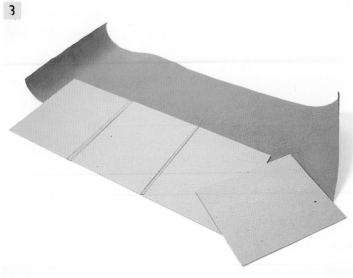

3 CUT THE BOARDS FOR THE CASE. Cut four pieces of binder's board:

Height = height of mats plus two board thicknesses
Width = width of mats plus two board thicknesses

From your scrap board, cut two joint spacers. Different spacers are required because, as the accordion closes, the first and the last joints must accommodate more bulk than the middle joint.
Spacer 1 (for first and last joints) = two binder's board thicknesses plus two mat thicknesses plus $^1/_{16}$" (.15 cm)
Spacer 2 (for middle joint) = two binder's board thicknesses

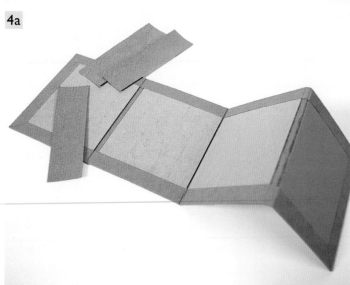

4a CONSTRUCT THE CASE. Cut a piece of Momi paper large enough to accommodate the four case boards and the joint spacers. Add a $^3/_4$" (2 cm) turn-in allowance around all four edges. Brush mixture onto the case boards and gently press them into position on the paper, leaving the proper joint spaces between the boards. Cut the corners (see The Basics, page 124). Applying your mixture sparingly, glue the head turn-in.

4b Bring the paper onto the boards and, with the edge of your bone folder, gently press the paper into the three joints. Pinch in the paper at the corners. Repeat with tail turn-in. Complete the spine and fore edge turn-ins.

CUT THREE HINGE STRIPS FROM THE MOMI PAPER.
Height = height of case boards minus $^1/_4$" (.5 cm)
Width = 2" (5 cm)

Stipple the mixture onto one hinge strip and, centering this strip, gently press the paper into the joints and onto the boards. Repeat with the other two hinges. Put the case aside to dry, flat, under a light weight.

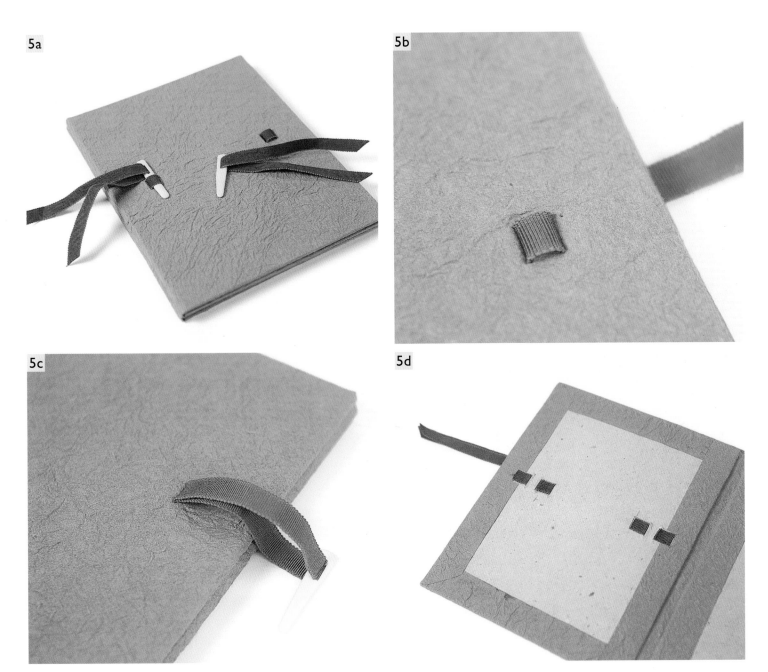

5a ATTACH THE BONE CLASPS.
Position the four mats on the case and close the case. Thread the ribbons through the slits in the bone clasps and place the clasps in the desired location on the front of the case. Mark the front of the case with four pinpricks, one on each side of the two clasps directly below their slits. (To make sure the clasps end up level with each other, make all marks on a pattern and then transfer these marks to your case.) Open up the case, remove the mats, and place the case right side up on a scrap board. Select a chisel to match the width of your ribbons.

Holding the chisel vertically, make four parallel chisel cuts (two per clasp), starting at the pinpricks and chiseling downward.

5b Angle the ends of two short pieces of ribbon and push down through the cuts, to form receiving loops for the clasps. Slide the clasps into the loops. Adjust the ribbons for a snug fit. Guide the main ribbons to the back of the case; mark for their insertion (again, with a pinprick or pattern). Make one vertical slit per ribbon.

5c Adjust the ribbons to make them taut. (Be sure the mats are inside the case

as you make these adjustments.) On the inside of the case, spread the ribbon ends in opposite directions.

5d With your knife, trace the outline of the ribbons, cutting and peeling up a shallow layer of board. Glue the ribbons into these recesses, using undiluted PVA. Make it as smooth as possible.

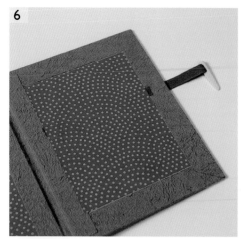

6

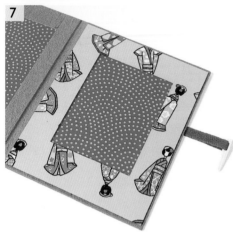

7

8

6 LINE THE CASE. Cut four pieces of decorative paper to fit within the case turn-ins. Paste out the papers and apply them to the case. Press the case, between newsprint and boards, under a light weight.

7 ATTACH THE MATS. The mats are glued to the case along three edges; the fourth edge is kept unglued, to allow for the insertion of the photographs. Glue backs of mats as follows (see diagram):

Mat 1: Glue out the head, tail, and the long edge of the mat that will sit near the outer edge of the case (i.e., away from the joint). Use undiluted PVA, masking off areas of the mat to be kept glue free with narrow strips of scrap paper. Brush the glue approximately $^1/_2$" (1 cm) onto the mats. Center the mat on the case board, pressing down along the edges with your bone folder. Carefully scoop away any seeping glue with a micro-spatula.

Mats 2 and 3: Glue out the head, tail, and the long edge of the mat that will sit near the middle joint. Continue as with mat 1.

Mat 4: Follow the process as with mat 1.

When all four mats have been glued to the case, press the case by placing it between newsprint and boards, and under a light weight.

8 CUT FOUR PIECES OF MYLAR, approximately 1" (3 cm) smaller than the mats in both height and width. Slide the Mylar under the mats. Insert photos under the Mylar.

Apply glue to shaded areas.

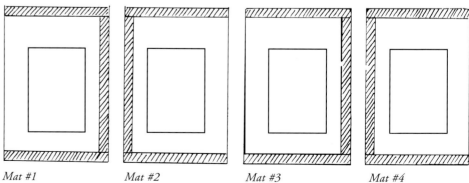

Mat #1 *Mat #2* *Mat #3* *Mat #4*

Tip: *How to Back Fabric*

MATERIALS

Cloth (lightweight cotton, handkerchief linen, silk)

Japanese tissue, such as mulberry paper

Paste (thick!)

Water, in a spritzer bottle

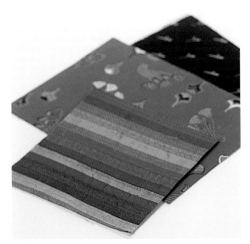

It is thrilling to transform special fabrics—a piece of a wedding dress, a quirky 1930s cotton print, an old silk scarf—into bookcloth. The method is simple, involving a bowl of paste and a sheet of Japanese paper. In contrast to the whimsically patterned silk used here, the case was lined with discarded pages from a botanical book found at a flea market.

1. Test your fabric for permanency of dyes. Wet a small piece. If the colors run, stop! Check out alternative backing techniques, such as those involving heat-set tissues.

2. Cut away the selvage from the fabric.

3. Cut a piece of Japanese tissue approximately 1" (3 cm) larger than the fabric on all four sides. Make sure the grain direction of fabric and paper is the same.

4. Place the fabric, right side down, on a non-porous surface (glass, Formica, Plexiglas). Spritz the cloth with water until it is fully saturated. Straighten the grain and smooth away wrinkles.

5. Paste out the sheet of Japanese tissue.

6. Hold a ruler over the short edge of the pasted paper, approximately $^{1}/_{2}$" (1 cm) and parallel with that edge. Give the ruler a quick press onto the paper. You are, briefly, pasting the ruler to the paper so that when you pick up the ruler the paper will adhere to it and be easily lifted off your workbench.

7. Lift and position the paper (pasted side down) on the fabric and slowly lower it onto the material. Don't place it down all at once, or you will trap huge air bubbles.

8. Draw a stiff dry brush across the surface of the paper, pressing to ensure a tight bond and to remove air bubbles.

9. Paste out the four edges of the paper that extend beyond the edges of the fabric. Stick down, onto one of these edges, a small piece (1"–2"; 3–5 cm) of heavyweight paper. This will become a lifting tab when the fabric has dried.

10. Carefully peel the backed fabric off your workbench and reverse it onto a drying surface. (Keep a sheet of Plexiglas in your studio for just this purpose. It can be put aside while the fabric is drying and not occupy valuable workbench space.) Make sure the four pasted edges are well adhered to the surface.

11. When the fabric has dried, slide the micro-spatula behind the paper tab and peel the fabric away from the board. Wash the drying surface with warm, soapy water.

The first scrapboard I ever saw was in a wonderful painting by the American trompe l'oeil master John Frederick Peto (1854–1907). A simple board crisscrossed with ribbons, it held letters and other ephemera and was an enchanting precursor to the modern bulletin board. My desk-sized version, encased in a portfolio, is a celebration of Victorian design. The bookcloth is embossed with a floral pattern, the ribbon is extravagant, and the tiers of pockets are cut from sheets of hand-marbled papers.

the victorian scrapboard...

organize your memories

MATERIALS

Binder's board
Bristol board (10 point)
Decorative paper; one
sheet 19" by 25"

(48 cm by 64 cm) is suffi-
cient for the scrapboard
pictured here
Bookcloth

Ribbon
PVA and mixture
Pressure-sensitive
adhesive (roll)

getting started:

- Collect the memorabilia for your scrapboard:
  letters, birth announcements, cards.
- Gather the decorative materials for your box.
  These can include decorative paper, ribbon,
  or swatches of fabric for pockets.

1a

1b

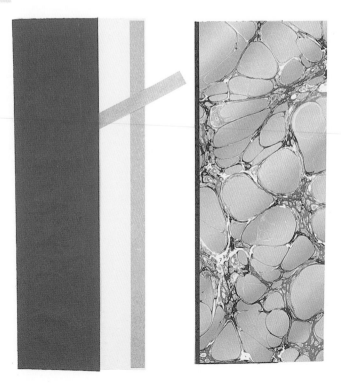

1a   CONSTRUCT THE SCRAPBOARDS.
Cut two pieces of binder's board to the
desired height and width. My boards are
12" by 10 ¹/₂" (30 cm by 27 cm).

Cut decorative paper into eight strips:
Height = 4" (10 cm) (adjust this measurement to accommodate pockets of different
depths)
Width = width of boards plus 2" (5 cm)

Cut bookcloth into six strips:
Height = 2¹/₂" (6 cm)
Width = width of boards plus 2" (5 cm)

Apply strips of pressure-sensitive adhesive
to the right side of the bookcloth, along
one long edge. Do not peel up the paper
backing. Apply strips of pressure-sensitive
adhesive to the wrong side of the decorative
paper, along both long edges. Do not peel up
paper backing. Apply a strip of pressure-
sensitive adhesive to the entire width of the
lower (tail) edge of each board. Do not
peel up paper backing.

1b   Adhere the decorative papers to the
bookcloth strips. Peel off the backing
paper from one edge of the decorative
paper. Press the paper onto the cloth,
approximately ¹/₈" (.3 cm) away from the
edge of the cloth without adhesive on it.
Roll back the paper, peel off the backing
strip from the cloth, and press the paper
onto the cloth. Repeat with the other five
strips. If your cloth tends to unravel, dip a
finger into the PVA and run it along the
exposed edge of cloth, sealing it. **Note:** The
photos illustrating Step 2 are of small scale
models of the actual scrapboards.

2a ASSEMBLE THE SCRAPBOARDS.
Place one of the two reserved decorative papers face down on the workbench. Remove the adhesive backing from the lower edge. Position the right side of the board (the side with the adhesive strip along its tail edge) on the paper, centered left to right and approximately 1" (3 cm) down from the head. Press.

2b Cut the corners, staying 1¹/₂ board thicknesses away from the tip of the board.

2c Apply adhesive to the two side (spine and fore-edge) turn-ins.

2d Bring the head turn-in onto the board and pinch in the corners.

2e Press the two side turn-ins onto the board.

2f To attach the first pocket, mark the board for its placement. Peel off the backing strip and stick down the pocket. Repeat with the second pocket. To adhere the third pocket, mark for its placement, remove the backing strip from the lower board edge, and stick down the pocket.

2g Turn the board over and complete the turn-ins. Starting with the upper pocket, apply strips of adhesive to the two side turn-ins; press them onto the board. Repeat with the second pocket. At the third pocket, first cut the corners and then bring in the long (tail) turn-ins before the two side ones.

2h–i Repeat Step 2 to complete the second scrapboard.

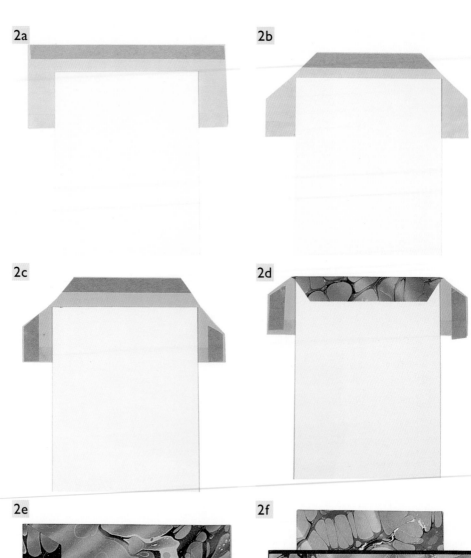

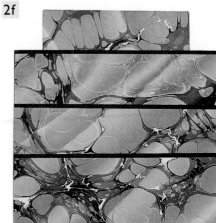

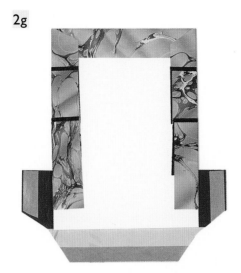

2g

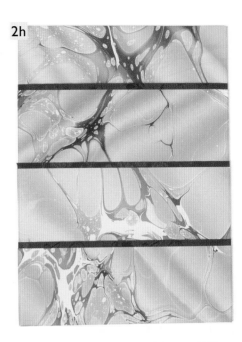

2h

NEXT   CUT OUT THE CASE UNITS.
The case is composed of three parts: front
and back, made of binder's board; and
spine, cut from the flexible (bristol) board.
There is no joint spacer. Pay attention to
the grain direction which runs, as always,
from head to tail.

CUT THE FRONT AND BACK CASE BOARD:

Height = height of scrapboards plus $1/4$"
(.5 cm)

Width = width of scrapboards plus $1/4$"
(.5 cm)

CUT THE SPINE PIECE:

Height = height of scrapboards plus $1/4$"
(.5 cm)

Width = thickness of the two scrapboards
plus two (case) board thicknesses plus two
cloth thicknesses, plus $1/8$" (.3 cm)

CUT THE BOOKCLOTH:

Height = height of case boards plus $1 1/2$"
(4 cm)

Width = width of case boards, laid out,
plus $1 1/2$" (4 cm)

2i

Make a pattern to determine the placement of the ties. Place the case, right side up, on a protected work surface. Transfer your placement mark to the case, and chisel. Repeat on the back board.

4b   Push the ribbons, with the help of your micro-spatula, through the slits and glue them into place.

3   CONSTRUCT THE CASE by gluing out the boards and adhering them to the cloth (see drawing). Cut the corners and complete the turn-ins (see The Basics, page 124).

Cut a hinge strip from the bookcloth:
Height = height of scrapboards
Width = width of spine piece plus 2" (5 cm)
Apply mixture to the cloth, center it on the spine, and press it firmly into place. Use your bone folder to sharply impress the edges of the case boards through the cloth.

Fill in the case. Cut two pieces of scrap paper large enough to fill in the area of exposed board on the inside of the case. Apply mixture to these papers and adhere them. This will counterbalance the pull of the boards toward the outside of the case. Put the finished case aside to dry, between newsprint sheets, under pressing boards and a weight.

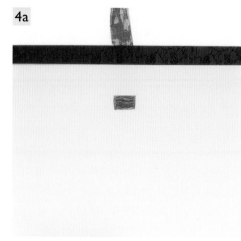

4a

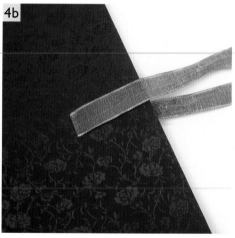

4b

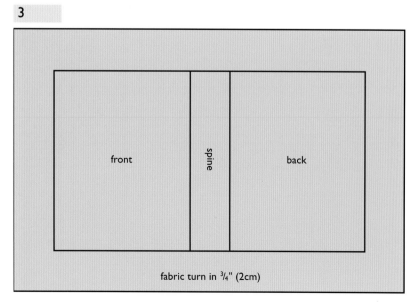

3

front

spine

back

grain

fabric turn in ³/₄" (2cm)

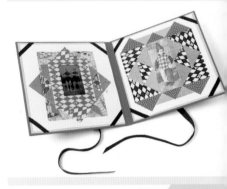

5

Ribbons can be used as fairly minimal corner restraints. They could also be glued diagonally, from side to side, across the entire surface of the board, creating the pineapple pattern in Peto's depictions.

5 GLUE THE SCRAPBOARDS TO THE CASE. Apply undiluted PVA to the wrong side of a scrapboard. Remove excess glue from the edges. Center the board on the case board and press it into position. Hold it for a minute or two, until the glue begins to set. Put newsprint, a pressing board, and a weight on top. Repeat these steps to attach the second scrapboard, making sure the pockets on both boards are facing in the same direction.

LEAVE THE FINISHED CASE under weights for several hours.

No glue! No paste! No complicated cuts! This box is, simply, two pieces of paper joined at the base with strips of pressure-sensitive adhesive. Since it is such an austere construction, The Paper Box needs a paper with character and body to give it charm. If the color is vibrant, this spunky box needs very little ornamentation: A button or two and a piece of bright thread are enough. The paper used here is a lustrous handmade. Its linen content gives the paper both strength and tactility. In this project you will use a new technique: scoring paper. This is a simple but important technique (see The Faux Book Box for an additional application), and deserves the highlighting starting on page 139.

the paper box...
for the love of paper

MATERIALS

A good-quality hand-made paper

Thread

Buttons

Elastic cord

Pressure-sensitive adhesive on a roll

PVA

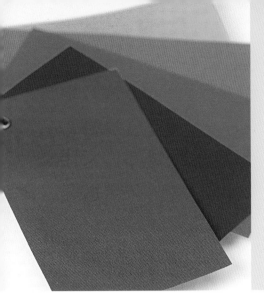

getting started:
cutting the first piece of paper

- Cut out the first piece to the following dimensions:
  Height = height of object to be boxed (referred to as "object" hereafter)
  Width = width of object, plus twice the thickness of the object, plus 2"–4" (5–10 cm), depending on the size of the box.
- If you intend to sew through the spine and fore-edge walls (as in the box pictured), increase this width measurement by approximately ¹/₄" (.5 cm) since the stitching on the inside of the box juts into the base, diminishing its overall width.

ONE

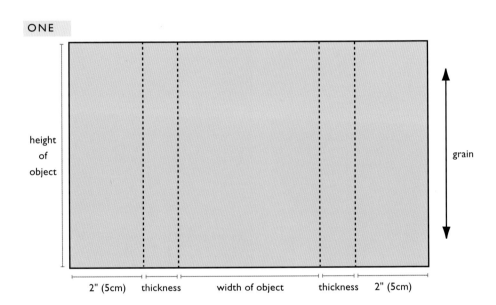

height
of
object

grain

2" (5cm) thickness width of object thickness 2" (5cm)

HOW TO SCORE A PIECE OF PAPER

Place a sheet of blotter, or a pad of newsprint, on your workbench. To make deep, crisp score marks, you must work on a cushioned surface.

Mark the paper for scoring. To mark, make small pinpricks with a sewing or potter's needle. (If you make pencil markings, you will need to erase them later.)

Place your triangle on the paper. The right angle of the triangle must sit on top of the pinprick. Draw a line with your bone folder, from the marked edge to its opposite edge (head to tail; spine to fore-edge). Keeping the triangle in place, scoot under the paper and run your folder up and down, pressing the paper firmly against the edge of the triangle. Remove the triangle. Fold over the paper and sharpen the crease with your folder.

Note: Steps 2 through 8 and Step 10 are illustrated with scale models of the actual box.

1 SCORE THE PAPER by centering the object on the paper and making two pinpricks, to the left and right of the object, on the tail edge of the paper. Score and sharply crease the paper. (See How to Score a Piece of Paper on page 139.)

2 FORM THE SPINE AND FORE-EDGE WALLS. Measure the thickness of the object and transfer this measurement to your paper, with pinprick markings, to the outside of the previously scored lines. (To measure for thickness, see The Basics, page 118.) Score and sharply crease the paper. Round the sharp corners, at head only.

3 CUT OUT THE SECOND PIECE:
Height = three times the height of the object plus twice its thickness
Width = width of object enclosed in the first piece
Grain must run from spine to fore-edge.

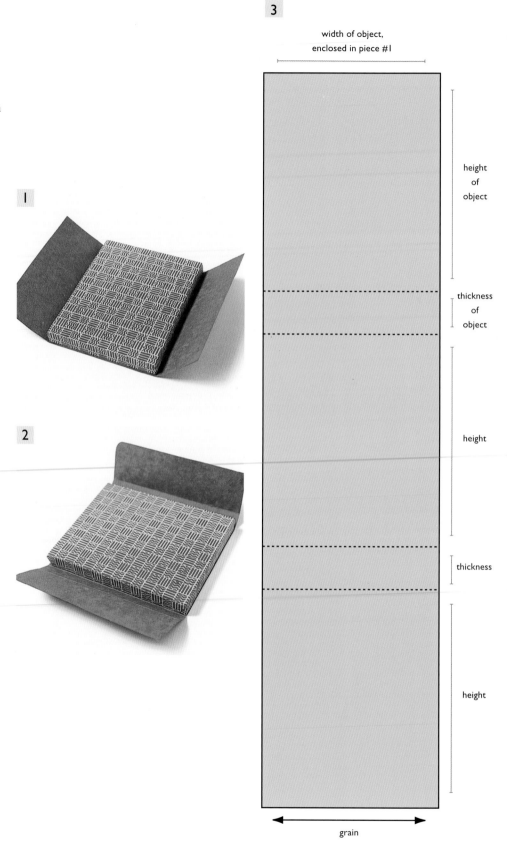

width of object, enclosed in piece #1

height of object

thickness of object

height

thickness

height

grain

4

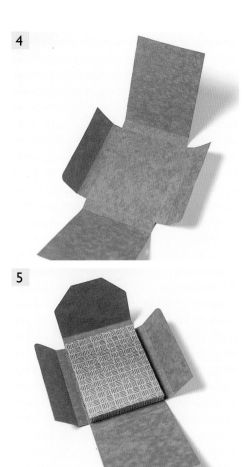

5

4   SCORE THE PAPER by centering the (enclosed) object on the paper and making two pinpricks, to the top and bottom of the object, on the spine edge of the paper. Score and sharply crease the paper.

From the head and tail walls. Measure the thickness of the object to be enclosed and transfer this measurement to your paper, with pinprick markings to the outside of the previously scored lines. Score and sharply crease the paper.

5   TRIM HEAD AND TAIL FLAPS to desired shape and depth. Round off all sharp edges on head flap.

6a   SEW ON BUTTON AND APPLY REINFOCEMENT PATCHES. Decide on the placement of the buttons and elastic cord on the head and tail flaps. Punch holes.

6b   Before sewing, cut and glue small patches of paper over punched area, either inside or out. Insert cord and sew on buttons.

6a

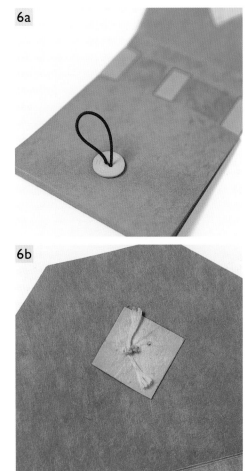

6b

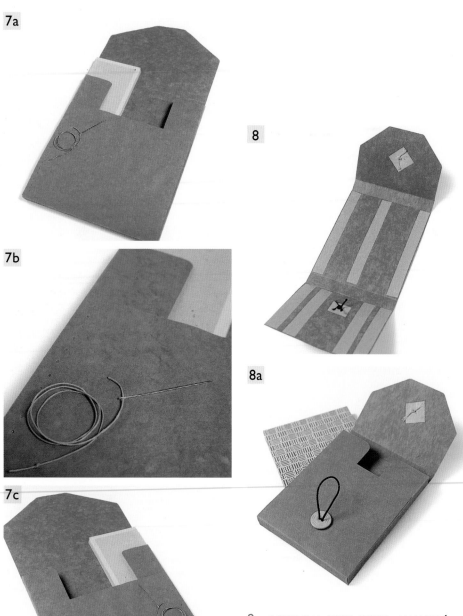

7a

7b

7c

8

8a

7a, b, c   If sewing the spine and fore-edge walls, punch holes through the tail flap, the flanges under the flap, and through corresponding areas on the spine and fore-edge walls. (See Tip on page 143.) Do not sew.

8   ATTACH THE TWO UNITS by applying strips of pressure-sensitive adhesive to the second piece, in the areas illustrated.

8a   Peel off backing paper on the base area only, and stick the two units together. If omitting decorative stitching, peel off backing paper on the tail flap and carefully align this flap with the spine and fore-edge flanges; press down into place.

8b   If sewing, thread two needles. Start on the inside of the tail flap, and sew toward the head in an overcast stitch, sewing up both sides simultaneously. When the sewing is complete, sneak inside and peel off backing paper on tail flap; press the flap onto the flange.

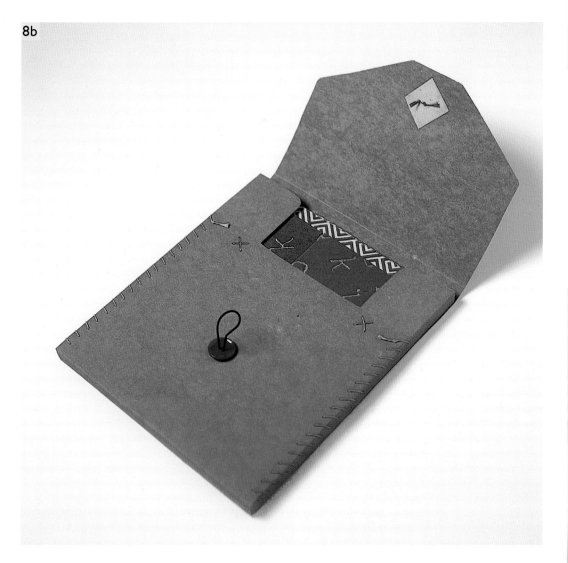

There are many ways to close this box. Apply ribbon ties, as in previous projects. Use adhesive-backed Velcro dots. Or, cut a slit in the tail flap and insert head flap into this slit.

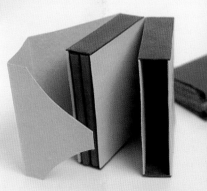

Tip *How to Punch Holes*

Make a punching block by taping scrap boards together, to the depth of your walls and to the appropriate height. To punch holes through the tail flap and the flanges underneath, insert this block into the box, align the papers in the proper position, and punch through both papers simultaneously. I held a ruler $1/4$" (.5 cm) away from the edge of the tail flap and punched holes at $1/2$" (1 cm) intervals. To make sure the holes in the two walls are in the corresponding positions, move the right angle of a triangle from hole to hole, punching holes in the wall as you go from head to tail.

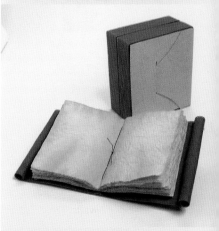

HEDI KYLE *Demosta*
5" x 4³/₈" x 2¹/₂"
(13cm x 11cm x 6cm) (closed)

books: Firenze paper soaked in coffee
box: Tim Barrett handmade and Moriki papers

The inspiration for this box is a poignant object from centuries ago. Made when the possession and reading of Tarot cards was a dangerous pursuit, this box was built to deceive. The titling on the spine is a clue to the contents, but the craftsmanship of this small beauty manages to hide its secrets. My box holds a collection of cards of another sort. In France, April Fool's Day is celebrated with fish: chocolate fish, pastry fish, paper fish. "Poissons d'Avril" fill this box.

The Faux Book Box is comprised of two units: An inner scored paper container and an outer case. If you intend to make the spine of your box resemble an old book, choose the covering material carefully. Select a strong but flexible handmade paper, and paint or stain it to look like leather. Accept the crinkles that will inevitably develop as the paper is molded over the fake raised bands. They are suggestive of a well-used, much-loved object.

the faux book box...
memories of second-hand bookshops

MATERIALS				
For the scored container:	A good-quality medium-weight paper	Decorative paper Paste	Pressure-sensitive adhesive on a roll
For the case:	Binder's board	Decorative paper	Cord
	Strong, flexible handmade paper (spine)	Bristol board, 10 point Headbands (optional)	PVA, mixture and paste

getting started:
select the paper for the laminate

- Cut one piece of medium-weight paper and two pieces of decorative paper to the same dimensions:
  Height = height of object to be boxed, plus two thicknesses of object, plus 1" (3 cm)
  Width = twice the width of the object, plus one thickness of object, plus 1" (3 cm)
- Make sure the grain runs from head to tail on all three papers.

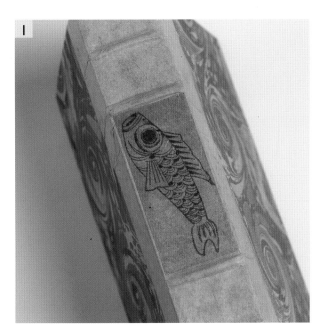

1 PREPARE THE LAMINATE
to become the scored-paper container. Dampen the plain paper with a wet sponge. Paste out the decorative papers (one at a time) and apply one to each side of the dampened paper. Press out air bubbles with your hands. Place this laminate between dry newsprint sheets, sandwich it between pressing boards, and leave it under weights for half an hour.

Cut the laminate to the following dimensions.

Height = height of object plus a hair, plus two thicknesses of object.
Width = twice the width of object, plus one thickness of object.

2a	2b	2c

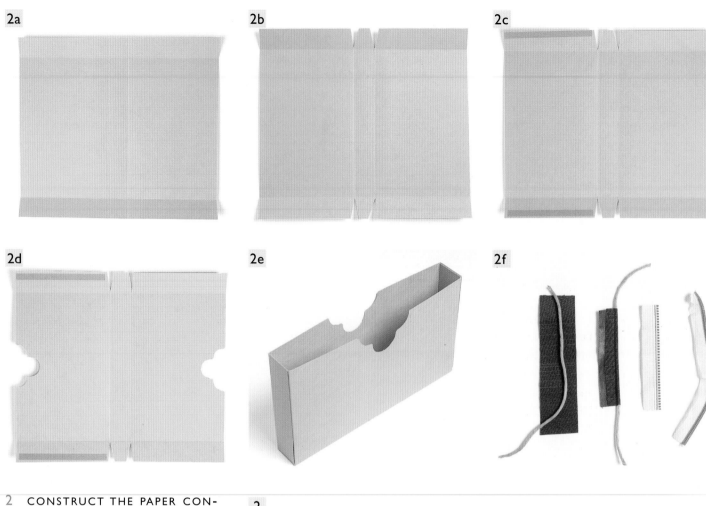

2d	2e	2f

2 CONSTRUCT THE PAPER CONTAINER.

The laminate *must* be scored while it is still damp. If it is dry, the against-the-grain folds are cracked and flaky. When using expensive materials, make a prototype out of cheap paper then transfer the measurements to the laminate.

2a Following the procedure for scoring paper described in The Paper Box (page 139); score the laminate.

2b Cut away triangular wedges.

2c On the left-hand panel (inside), apply strips of pressure-sensitive adhesive close to the outer edges of the head and tail turn-ins. Repeat on the right-hand panel, applying the adhesive to the reverse (outside) of the laminate.

2d Make thumb cuts on the fore-edges, of desired size and design.

2e Fold up the box and stick the turn-ins together, tucking the spine tab in between the two long turn-ins.

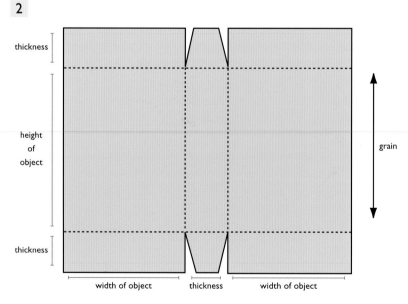

2f **Optional:** Glue endbands (available from bookbinding suppliers, or made by gluing fabric around a piece of cord) to head and tail, at spine. The bands are cut to the exact thickness of the box spine.

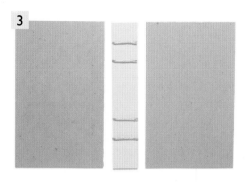

3 CUT OUT THE CASE BOARDS.

The front and back boards are cut from binder's board:

Height = height of box, plus two board thicknesses

Width = width of box, plus one board thickness

The spine is cut from 10 point bristol board:

Height = height of box, plus two board thicknesses

Width = thickness of box, plus two (case) board thicknesses, plus slightly more than two spine paper thicknesses

Optional: To make fake raised bands, glue strips of cord across the spine board, at desired intervals. If you plan to label your box, space these bands accordingly.

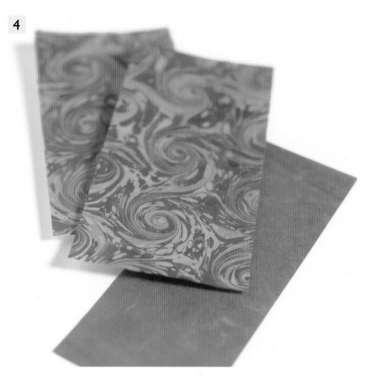

4 CUT OUT THE COVERING MATERIALS.

Cut one piece of strong but thin and resilient handmade paper to cover the spine:

Height = height of boards, plus 1 1/2" (4 cm)

Width = desired width—from front board, across spine, to back board

Cut two pieces of decorative paper to cover the boards:

Height = height of boards, plus 1 1/2" (4 cm)

Width = distance from edge of spine paper to fore-edge of board plus 1" (3 cm)

5a

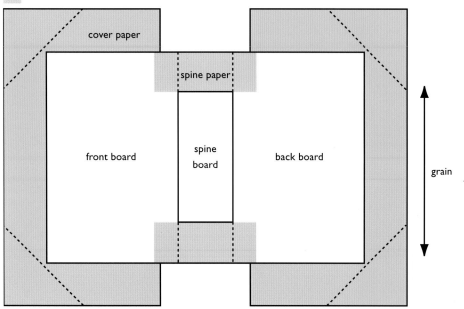

cover paper

spine paper

front board

spine board

back board

grain

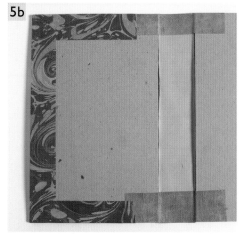

5b

5c

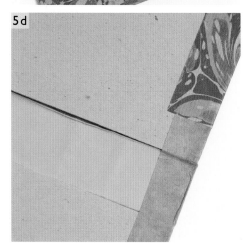

5d

5 ASSEMBLE THE CASE
(see diagram.)

5a Paste out the spine paper. Center the spine piece (cord side down) on the paper. Flip the spine over onto a piece of wax paper. Mold the paper around the cords, sliding the paper down from the head and tail to provide ample material to stretch around the cords. Moisten the paper with a sponge and continue to work it around the cords with your bone folder, until the hubs are well-defined. Turn the spine over, onto a piece of newsprint, and re-apply paste to the head, tail, and spine extensions. Place the front and back boards on the paper, snugly abutting the spine board. Bring in the head and tail turn-ins. Turn the case over and carefully try to smooth out the wrinkles. Don't be too obsessive: They are inevitable and they contribute to the old-book look.

5b–d Paste out the decorative papers and apply them to the boards. These papers should overlap the spine paper by a small margin. Cut the corners and finish the edges (see The Basics, page 124).

Cut the inner hinge strip from the spine covering paper:
Height = height of paper box
Width = width of case spine board, plus 2" (5 cm)

Do not paste this strip to the case.

6 ATTACH THE BOX TO THE CASE.
Glue the spine of the box with undiluted PVA, taking care not to stain the endbands. With your finger, remove any excess glue. Stick the right side of the hinge strip onto the spine, centering it head to tail and left to right.

6a, b   Rub it down well. Paste out the entire back of the hinge strip and center the box on the spine of the case. Use your bone folder to force the hinge sharply against the spine edges of the case boards. Press the paper onto the boards. Keeping the box in an upright position, fill it with scrap boards cut to fit. This will help press the box to the case.

NEXT   **LINE THE CASE.** Cut two pieces of decorative paper:
Height = height of paper box
Width = width of case boards, minus two board thicknesses
(Remember to anticipate the stretch of the paper in width, and trim it a bit narrower if necessary.)

Paste out these papers and apply them. With the case remaining in this open position, stack newsprint, pressing boards and weights on top of each board, and let dry.

7 LABEL THE BOX. Using a pen, paintbrush, rubber stamp or computer, generate artwork for the label. Draw or print it on a contrasting paper. Paste the label to the spine, between the bands.

6a

6b

7

VARIATION

The marbled paper used on this box is a contemporary Italian marble based on a traditional pattern. Old book papers can also be retrieved and reused on new book and box projects. Scavenge around second-hand bookstores for discarded covers. Take them home and let them soak in a bathtub filled with warm water. As the adhesive dissolves, the papers will loosen and peel away from the boards. If this doesn't happen, keep adding hot water to the bath, and gently pull the papers away from the boards. Remove the papers and blot them with paper towels. Place them right side up on wax paper (in case of a sticky residue). Sandwich the papers between blotters, pressing boards, and weights until dry.

If the papers seem too fragile for re-use, paste them onto sheets of Japanese tissue while still damp, and press as above.

Sometimes, the best surprises are the unexpected ones. As the marbled papers float off the boards, printed "waste sheets"—magazine pages, handwritten account-book pages, a sheet of music—appear below. Used as board liners, these sheets can also be retrieved with additional soaking time.

Creative ideas—whether watercolor paintings or sketches for a new craft project—deserve a special home. You won't find a more wonderful home for your work than The Artist's Portfolio.

And just as the artwork deserves a special place, so does your portfolio deserve a label. Labels enliven objects, identify their contents, and help to distinguish the fronts from the backs. In this case, the artist is a wonderful calligrapher, Anna Pinto. To protect the paper label, cut away several layers of the cover board, creating a well into which the label can be dropped. The cutaway area is slightly larger than Anna's art-work. The result is a shadow that frames the artwork.

The Artist's Portfolio consists of a case with three separately constructed flaps. Keep the outside plain, to highlight the unique contents. But there is a surprise when you open this box: Here is one portfolio that will never be mistaken for a standard art-supply-store item.

the artist's portfolio...
preserve your memories

MATERIALS	Binder's board (case)	Bookcloth	PVA, mixture and paste
	Museum board, two or	Decorative paper	Artwork for cover
	four ply (flaps)	Ribbon	

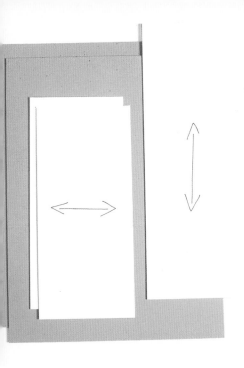

getting started:
cutting the boards

- Cut out the front and back case boards:
  Height = height of material to be boxed, plus ¹/₂" (1 cm)
  Width = width of material to be boxed, plus ¹/₄" (.5 cm)
- Cut out the boards for the flaps:
  Head and tail flaps: cut two
  Height = 4" (10 cm), or desired height
  Width = width of material to be boxed, plus ¹/₈" (.3 cm)
  Fore-edge flap: cut one
  Height = height of material to be boxed, plus ¹/₄" (.5 cm)
  Width = 4" (10 cm), or desired width, matched to height of
  head and tail flaps
- Grain should run from head to tail on all boards.

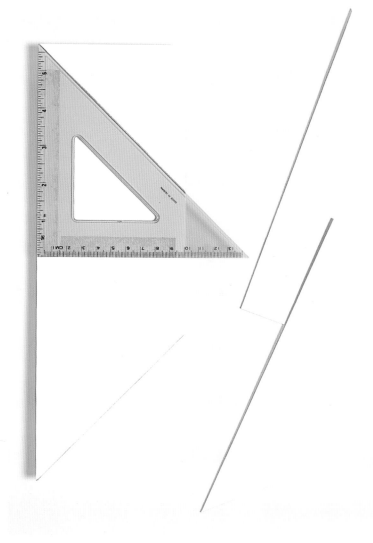

I **MITER THE CORNERS** of the flaps. Using a 45-degree triangle, draw and cut off one wedge from each head and tail flap, and two wedges from the fore-edge flap.

2a–f **CONSTRUCT THE FLAPS.**
For the head and tail flaps, cut two pieces of cloth:
Height = height of board, plus the thickness of the material to be boxed, plus 1³/₄" (4.5 cm)
Width = width of board, plus 1¹/₂" (4 cm)
For the fore-edge flap, cut one piece of cloth:
Height = height of board, plus 1¹/₂" (4 cm)
Width = width of flap, plus the thickness of the material to be boxed, plus 1³/₄" (4.5 cm)
Glue out the boards using mixture and stick them onto the cloth. *Pay attention: The head and tail flaps are mirror images and must be glued in opposite orientations.* Note that the untrimmed long edge of each board sits near a generous cloth extension. This cloth—the thickness of the material to be boxed, plus 1" (3 cm)—will eventually become the walls of the portfolio and the hinge attachment of the flaps to the case.

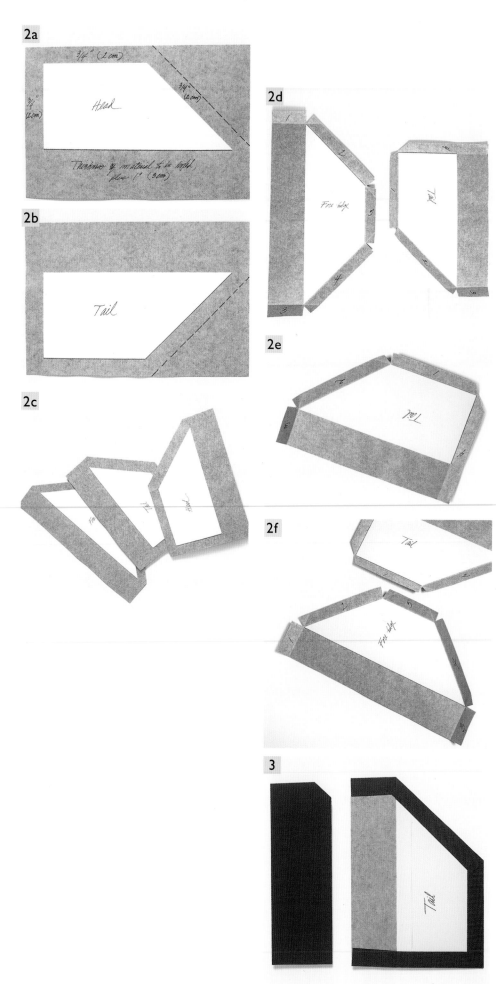

2a

3/4" (2 cm)

3/4" (2cm)

3/4" (2cm)

Head

Thickness of material to be boxed, plus 1" (3 cm)

2b

Tail

2c

Fore

Tail

Head

2d

Fore edge

Tail

2e

Tail

2f

Tail

Fore edge

3

Tail

Trim cloth near the angled edges of the boards, as illustrated, to create the usual 3/4" (2 cm) turn-in. Cut corners and finish all edges except the long edge, which will become the hinge attachment to the case. To cleanly cover the angled edges of the flaps, remove triangular bits of cloth. Crease and re-crease the turn-ins in all possible sequences to determine which bits to cut. When cutting, end cuts 1 1/2" board thicknesses away from the boards. Glue the turn-ins in the labeled sequence.

3 CUT THE INNER HINGE STRIPS for all three flaps. For the head and tail flaps, cut two strips of cloth:

Height = thickness of the material to be boxed, plus 1 3/4" (4.5 cm)

Width = width of flap, minus two board thicknesses

For the fore-edge flap, cut one strip of cloth:

Height = height of flap, minus two board thicknesses

Width = thickness of the material to be boxed, plus 1 3/4" (4.5 cm)

Before gluing, place the hinge strips in the proper position on the flaps, and cut off the corners that extend beyond the angled edges. With pencil, mark each flap approximately 3/4" (2 cm) away from its long edge. Apply mixture to the hinge strips (one at a time). Starting on the 3/4" (2 cm) markings, press the cloth onto the board. Push the cloth sharply against the board edge with your folder. Press the extending cloth onto the fabric below. Don't stop pressing until the two are well bonded. Sandwich this hinge between newsprint, pressing boards, and weights until dry. To even out the raw edges of this hinge extension, trim a uniform amount of cloth off each of the three flaps.

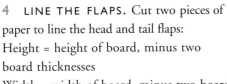

4 **LINE THE FLAPS.** Cut two pieces of paper to line the head and tail flaps:
Height = height of board, minus two board thicknesses
Width = width of board, minus two board thicknesses
Cut one piece of paper to line the fore-edge flap:
Height = height of board, minus two board thicknesses
Width = width of board, minus two board thicknesses
Before gluing, place the lining papers in the proper position on the flaps and cut off the corners that extend beyond the angled edges. Apply adhesive to the papers and stick them down. Put flaps aside to dry, between newsprint sheets and under boards and a weight.

5 **FORM THE FLAP WALLS.** From your scrap board, cut a strip equal to the thickness of the material to be boxed; this is your wall spacer (Spacer 1). To form the head, tail, and fore-edge walls, push this spacer firmly against the long edge of each flap and crease the fabric hinge to form a right angle. On the head and tail flaps only, trim a wedge off the cloth hinge near the spine edge. Put the flaps aside.

6a

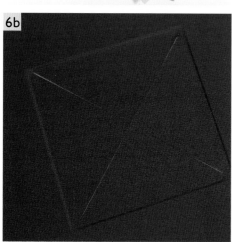

6b

6a   CONSTRUCT THE CASE. Decide on the placement of the cover artwork. Cut and peel away layers of board equal to the thickness of the artwork (See Tip on page 66). Cut the spine spacer from a strip of scrap board. The width of this spacer is the thickness of the flap spacer, plus two (case) board thicknesses, plus the thickness of one flap, plus two cloth thicknesses.

Cut a piece of bookcloth to cover case:
Height = height of boards, plus 1 1/2" (4 cm)
Width = width of boards laid out with spacer in place, plus 1 1/2" (4 cm)
Glue out the front board. Draw away excess glue with your brush from around the edges of the label recess. Make sure that no small bits of cardboard are stuck to the surface. Place this board on the left-hand side of the cloth, centered on height and with a 3/4" (2 cm) margin on your left. Press the board down. Turn the cloth over immediately and, working through a sheet of scrap paper, press out all air bubbles with your folder. Find the edges of the cut-away area and shape the cloth sharply against these edges.

6b   If your cloth is stubborn and refuses to stretch, cut an X in the middle of the recessed area; start and end the cuts approximately 1/4" (.5 cm) away from the corners. As you shape the cloth against the edges, be careful not to smear the glue. Once shaped, flip the case over, place the spine spacer next to the cover board, glue out the back board, and put it down. Press, then remove the spacer and turn the case over. Press the cloth down well, working first with your hands and then with your folder. Flip the case back to its original position, cut the corners, and finish the edges (see The Basics, page 124).

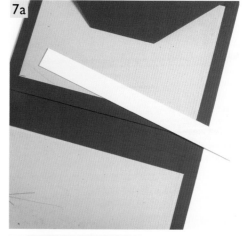

7a

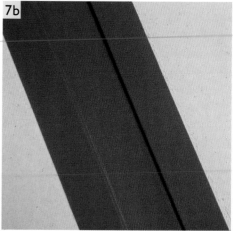

7b

7   CUT AND APPLY THE SPINE HINGE STRIP.

7a   Cut a piece of cloth:
Height = height of case minus 1/4" (.5 cm)
Width = width of spine spacer plus 2" (5 cm)
Apply mixture to this hinge and center it on the spine.

7b   Rub vigorously, forcing the fabric against the board edges. Trim a hair off the spine spacer in width, and re-position it in the spine area. With a weight on top, it will press both cloths together. Let sit for half an hour to one hour.

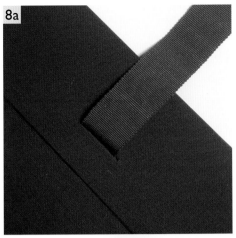

8a

8b

8a ATTACH THE RIBBON TIES.
Decide on the placement of the ties. (If you wish to center them, cut a scrap of paper to the height of the case and fold it in half. Voila! The center.) Mark this area with a pinprick. Select a chisel the width of your ribbon. Chisel, vertically, from the outside of the case. Be sure to protect your tabletop before chiseling. Repeat on the back board.

8b Insert the ribbons into these slits and pull them to the inside of the case. Cut and peel up a shallow layer of board and glue the ribbon ends with undiluted PVA, sinking them into the recess.

9

9 GLUE THE FLAPS TO THE BACK OF THE CASE. Use undiluted PVA, and start with the fore-edge flap. Masking the walls with a piece of scrap paper, glue out the hinge. Remove excess glue, taking care not to smear glue onto the wall area. Center the flap by height on the case; it should sit just inside the board edge of the case. Press down well with your folder. Repeat with the head and tail flaps, positioning the flaps flush with the spine edge of the case. To reduce bulk at the outer corners where the head and tail flaps overlap the fore-edge flap, miter the corners after gluing. To miter, make a diagonal cut through both hinges simultaneously, drawing the knife from the right angle formed at the outer overlapping area to the right angle formed at the inner overlapping area. You will need to peel up the head and tail flaps slightly, to remove the triangular wedge from the fore-edge flap underneath. Re-apply a dot of adhesive, if necessary, and stick back down.

NEXT LINE THE CASE.
Cut two pieces of paper:
Height = height of case, minus two board thicknesses
Width = width of case, minus two board thicknesses
The lining for the back board might need to be trimmed; check the fit before gluing. Apply adhesive to these papers and stick them down. Place newsprint, boards, and weights on the case, and let sit until dry.

NEXT APPLY ARTWORK TO COVER.
Apply appropriate adhesive to artwork, and stick down into cover recess. Remember to anticipate the expansion of wet paper, and trim accordingly. When setting in a photograph or artwork involving water-based inks, use a moisture-free (pressure-sensitive) adhesive.

Tip: How to Prepare a Cover Board for a Label

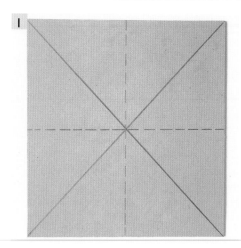

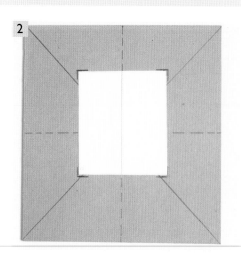

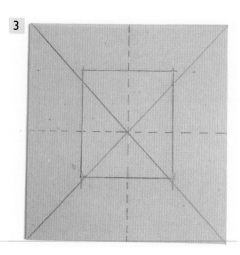

1. Cut a paper pattern:

Height = height of artwork, plus $1/8$" (.3 cm)

Width = width of artwork, plus $1/8$" (.3 cm)

(The pattern is larger than the artwork to allow for a shadow around it once it is glued into place.) Crease this pattern in half, both vertically and horizontally, to find the center.

NEXT Draw diagonal lines, from corner to corner, on your cover board. Using your triangle to maintain right angles, draw a line from head to tail, through the bisecting point. Draw a second line, from spine to fore-edge, through the bisecting point.

2. Place the paper pattern on the board, aligning its creased lines with the drawn lines. Slide the pattern up and down and side to side to decide on the placement of your artwork. Or keep it right where it is at dead center.

NEXT Trace the outline of the pattern on the board.

3. Using your triangle and a knife with a sharp blade, cut through the pattern's lines. Make several cuts over the same area before proceeding from one line to the next.

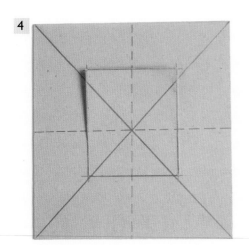

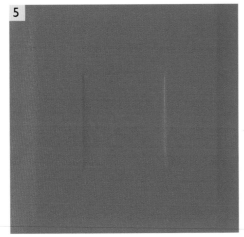

4. Use the tip of the blade to dig under and lift up the board in one corner. Grab this corner and peel up several layers of board with the help of the knife. Peel and lift in the direction of the grain. Clean up the corners by scraping with your knife. Make sure the edges are crisp.

NEXT Smooth the cut-away surface by rubbing vigorously with your folder. Also smooth down the roughed-up outer edges of the cut-away.

5. Glue out the board and position it on the cloth. Flip the board over and immediately find the edge of the recess with your hands. (Work through a newsprint sheet to protect the surface of the cloth.) Work out all air bubbles, puncturing the cloth with a sewing needle, if necessary. Shape the cloth sharply against the edges of the recess with a tapered bone folder.

6. If the cloth is stubborn and refuses to mold itself against the edges of the cut-away, make two diagonal slits through the cloth, starting and ending the slits at least $1/8$" (.3 cm) away from the corners.

Its charm is in its size (2¹/₂" [6 cm] square), as well as in its materials. Several small boxes, stacked or scattered, have more presence than one large and lonely box. So make lots of boxes—and let them become your jewels!

The Jewelry Box consists of two units: a four-walled tray and a case. The case extends slightly beyond the edges of the tray, creating a small lip. Once assembled, the front of the case becomes the hinged lid of the box.

Keep in mind the rules of boxmaking: Wherever hinging occurs, use cloth instead of paper. The one exception is in the use of Momi papers (please see my note in The Picture Frame Box on page 127). If not using these resilient Japanese papers, I use bookcloth for the case construction. In the directions, the case material is referred to as cloth.

the jewelry box...
memories of treasures and trinkets

MATERIALS	Binder's board	Cloth or paper (tray)	Ribbon
	Museum board, two ply (liners)	Cloth or Momi paper (case)	PVA, mixture and paste
		Bone clasp	

getting started: cutting the boards

- Cut out the boards for the tray following the layout shown.
- Pay attention to the logic of the cuts, which ensures that all parts sharing the same measurements are cut in sequence, and with a minimum of marking.
- Base:

  Height = desired height of tray, plus two covering thicknesses

  Width = desired width of tray, plus two covering thicknesses
- Head and tail walls:

  Height = desired depth of tray, plus one board thickness

  Width = desired width of tray, plus two covering thicknesses
- Spine and fore-edge walls:

  Height = height of base board, plus two board thicknesses

  Width = desired depth of tray, plus one board thickness

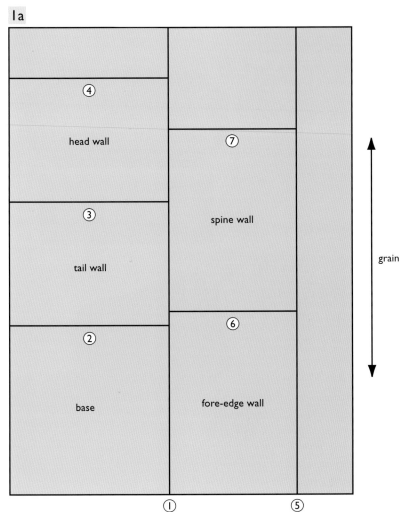

1a

④

head wall

③

tail wall

⑦

spine wall

②

base

⑥

fore-edge wall

①   ⑤

grain

1b

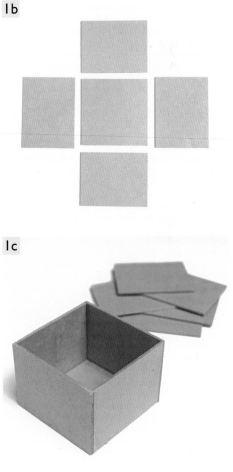

1c

1a–c   CONSTRUCT THE TRAY
(see The Basics, page 122.) Glue the walls in the proper sequence: head, fore-edge, tail, spine.

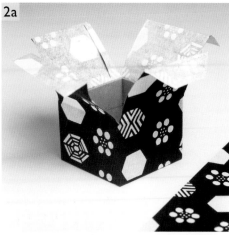

2a

2b

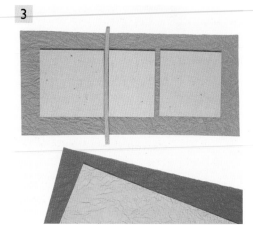

3

2a COVER THE TRAY. Cut out the covering material, a strip twice the depth of the tray plus 1 1/2" (4 cm), and long enough to wrap around all four walls plus 1/2" (1 cm). If the material is too short to wrap around the tray in one continuous strip, piece together two shorter strips, making sure that the seam falls on a corner of the tray.

2b Cover the tray (see The Basics, page 122).

3 CUT OUT THE THREE CASE BOARDS to the following dimensions. Remember that the grain must run from head to tail on all boards.
Front and Back:
Height = height of tray, plus two board thicknesses
Width = width of tray, plus one board thickness
Spine:
Height = height of tray, plus two board thicknesses
Width = depth of tray (Here's an easy and accurate way to get this measurement: Sharply crease a small piece of scrap paper to form a right angle; place the tray on top of this paper and push the tray snugly into the right angle; make a second, parallel crease, over the top of the tray. The distance between these two crease marks is the exact depth of your tray.)

From your scrap board, cut a slender strip a scant two board thicknesses in width. This will be used as a spacer when gluing up the case.

NEXT   CUT OUT THE CASE CLOTH or Momi paper:
Height = height of boards, plus 1 1/2" (4 cm)
Width = width of boards, laid out with joint spacer plus 1 1/2" (4 cm)

4 CONSTRUCT THE CASE. Glue out the front board and place it on the cloth, approximately 3/4" (2 cm) away from all three edges. Press into place. Position the spacer against the spine edge of the board, glue the spine piece, position the spine on the cloth, and push it firmly against the spacer. Remove the spacer and place it on the other side of the spine. Glue the back board, position it on the cloth pushed firmly against the spacer, and press into place.

5 CUT THE CORNERS and finish the edges. Cut the inner hinge cloth:
Height = height of the tray
Width = width of case spine, plus 2" (5 cm)
Grain, as always, runs from head to tail. Cut shallow triangular wedges off all four corners of this cloth.

6 GLUE OUT THE HINGE CLOTH, cen-

4

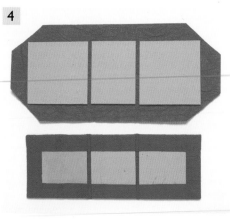

5

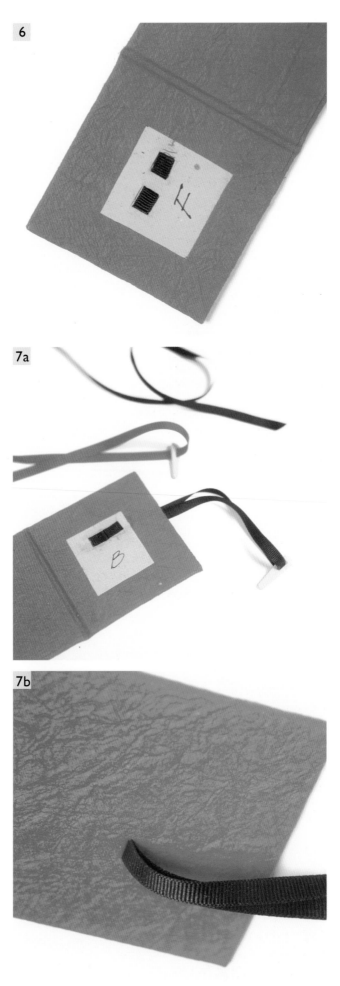

6 GLUE OUT THE HINGE CLOTH, center it on the spine, press the cloth firmly into the joints of the case with your bone folder, then onto the front and back case boards. Rub down well.

7a ATTACH THE BONE CLASP. Feed the ribbon through the slit in the bone clasp. Place the tray in the case, close it, and position the bone clasp on the front of the case, in its desired location. (If making more than one box, prepare patterns for the placement of the ribbons on both front and back.) Mark the front of the case with two pinpricks, one on each side of the clasp directly below its slit. Remove the tray and arrange the case right side up on a piece of scrap board. Select a chisel to match the width of your ribbon. Holding the chisel vertically make two parallel chisel cuts, starting at the pinpricks and chiseling downward.

7b Angle the ends of a short piece of ribbon and push the ribbon down through the cuts to form a receiving loop for the clasp. Slide the clasp into the loop. Pull the ribbon ends snugly on the inside of the case. Guide the main ribbon to the back of the case; mark for its insertion and make one vertical slit. Feed both ends of the ribbon into this slit, and make the ribbon taut. On the inside of the case, spread the ribbon ends in opposite directions. With your knife trace the outlines of the ribbons, cutting and peeling up a shallow layer of board. Glue the ribbons into these recesses using undiluted PVA. Bone down this area well to make it as smooth as possible.

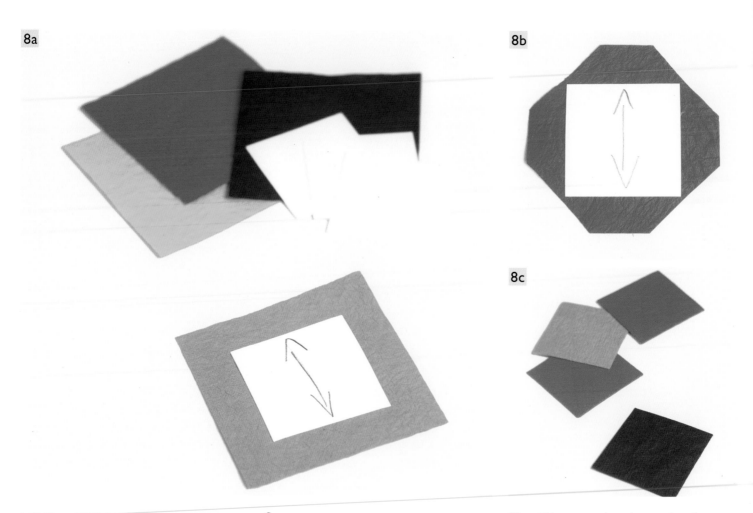

NEXT **ATTACH THE TRAY TO THE CASE.** Spread undiluted PVA onto the bottom of the tray; wipe away excess glue. Place the tray on the back case board. The spine edge of the case should be flush with the spine edge of the tray. Center the tray by height. This placement allows a small lip around the head, fore-edge, and tail. Hold the tray in position for a few minutes, until the glue begins to set. (Take care to keep the tray centered—it's quite a slippery creature at first!) Invert the case, place a board and hefty weight on top, and press for at least a half hour.

Spread undiluted PVA onto the spine wall of the tray; wipe away excess glue. Roll the tray onto the case, spine walls touching; slide a board and a weight into the tray, and press until dry.

8   LINE THE BOX.

8a   If lining with a medium or heavy-weight paper, cut two pieces of paper to the same dimensions. (Remember to anticipate the stretch of the paper across the grain, and to cut it a bit narrower in width.)

Height = height of interior of tray, minus two paper thicknesses

Width = width of interior of tray, minus two paper thicknesses

Paste the papers and apply them to the bottom of the tray and the inside of the box lid. Press until dry.

8b   If lining with a thin or fragile paper or with cloth, first "card" the material around lightweight boards, following the procedure below.

Cut out two pieces of museum board:

Height = height of interior of tray, minus $1/16$" (0.15 cm)

Width = width of interior of tray, minus $1/16$" (0.15 cm)

8c   Cut out two pieces of covering paper:

Height = height of boards, plus $1 1/2$" (4 cm)

Width = width of boards, plus $1 1/2$" (4 cm)

Paste the papers, center the board on the papers, cut the corners and finish the edges.

Glue out one board with undiluted PVA and carefully lower it into the tray. Press until it takes hold. If your box is large, place newsprint, a board and a weight on top, and let sit for half an hour. Glue out the second board, and center it on the box lid. Press until it takes hold. Weight and let sit for one half to one hour.

Tip: How to Make a Ribbon from Bookcloth

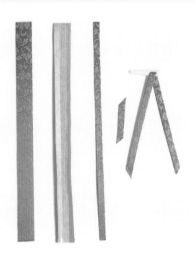

1. Cut a piece of bookcloth a scant ³/₄" (2 cm) in width and twice the desired length, plus 2" (5 cm). Grain must run lengthwise. Use your spring divider to divide this strip into ¹/₄" (.5 cm) increments (lengthwise).

2. Score the fabric into thirds. To score, position the cloth wrong side up on a piece of blotter. Working against a metal straight-edge with a tapered bone folder, "draw" two parallel lines ¹/₄" (.5 cm) apart from head to tail. Crease the fabric firmly along these score lines.

3. With your small brush, apply mixture to the cloth, starting in the middle of the fabric and working the adhesive toward the ends. Do not over glue. Turn the edges of the strip in toward the center of the fabric—first one, then the other—pressing with your fingers as you go. Place the strip between two waste sheets and press well with your bone folder. Let sit, between pressing boards and under weights until ready to use.

To close this little brocade box, make a ribbon from book cloth. This is an elegant alternative to store-bought ribbon when using bone clasps as closures on an all-cloth project.

My mother's button "box" was actually a large glass jar filled to the brim with a glorious mixture of buttons. When we were sick we sorted the buttons by color and size. When well, and playing pirates, we poured buttons over the carpet and reveled in our "pieces of eight." In homage to that jar, The Button Box is a true treasure chest full of plastic bounty. It even depends on buttons for its finial and feet embellishments. The Button Box is composed of a four-walled tray mounted on a platform, and a removable lid.

the button box...
memories of once-treasured garments

MATERIALS	Binder's board	Ribbon	PVA, mixture and paste
	Museum board, two-ply	Buttons	Epoxy or wood glue
	Assorted decorative	Thread	(optional)
	papers		

getting started: cutting the boards

- Cut out the boards for the tray, following the layout below.
- Base:

  Height = desired height of tray, plus two covering thicknesses

  Width = desired width of tray, plus two covering thicknesses
- Head and tail walls:

  Height = desired depth of tray, plus one board thickness

  Width = desired width of tray, plus two covering thicknesses

  (same as width of base board)
- Spine and fore-edge walls:

  Height = height of base board, plus two board thicknesses

  Width = desired depth of tray, plus one board thickness

  (same as height of head and tail walls)

1a–c CONSTRUCT THE TRAY
(see The Basics, page 122). Glue the walls in the proper sequence: head, fore-edge, tail, spine.

1a

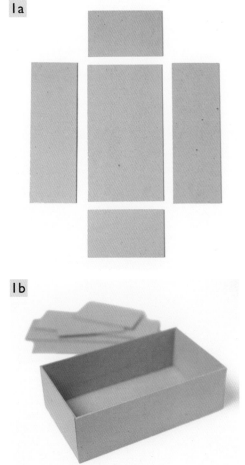

1b

1c

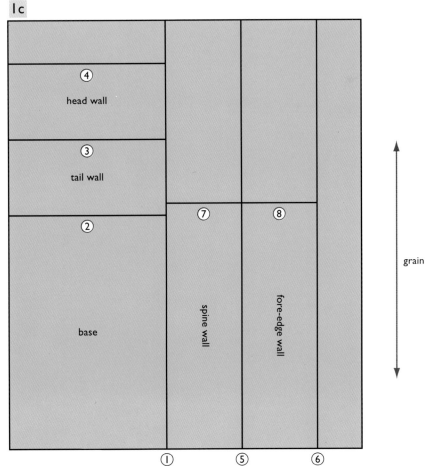

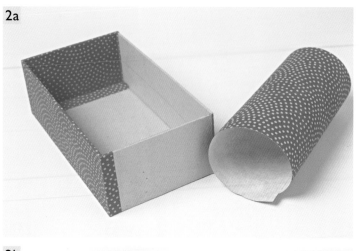

2a

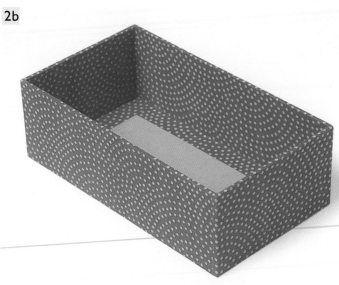

2b

2 COVER THE TRAY.

2a   Cut out the covering paper, a strip twice the depth of the tray plus 1 1/2" (4 cm), and long enough to wrap around all four walls plus 1/2" (1 cm). If the paper is too short to wrap around the tray in one continuous strip, piece together two papers, making sure that the seam falls on a corner of the tray.

2b   Cover the tray (see The Basics, page 123).

3 CONSTRUCT THE LID AND THE BASE PLATFORM. Cut out two boards to the same measurements:

Height = height of tray, plus two board thicknesses

Width = width of tray, plus two board thicknesses

Cut two pieces of decorative paper to the same measurements:

Height = height of boards, plus 1 1/2" (4 cm)

Width = width of boards, plus 1 1/2" (4 cm)

Cover the boards by pasting the papers and centering the boards on them. Cut the corners and finish the edges (see The Basics, page 124). Fill in the exposed area of the board with scrap paper. Put the boards aside to dry between newsprint sheets and pressing boards, and under weights.

3

4 CONSTRUCT THE LID LINER. This board, glued to the inside of the lid, keeps the lid anchored to the tray. Cut one board:

Height = height of interior of tray, minus two paper thicknesses

Width = width of interior of tray, minus two paper thicknesses

Cut one piece of decorative paper:

Height = height of board, plus 1 1/2" (4 cm)

Width = width of board, plus 1 1/2" (4 cm)

Cover and fill in this board, following the procedure described above. Put it aside to dry.

5 DECORATE THE TRAY. Cut two lengths of ribbon, long enough to wrap around the tray plus 2" (5 cm). Starting 1" (3 cm) in from one end, sew on buttons. Avoid placing buttons where the ribbon folds around the corners. Glue the ribbon with undiluted PVA—one wall length at a time—and stretch it around the tray, pressing with your bone folder as each wall is covered. Hide the raw ends of the ribbons by overlapping and tucking under the leftover bits.

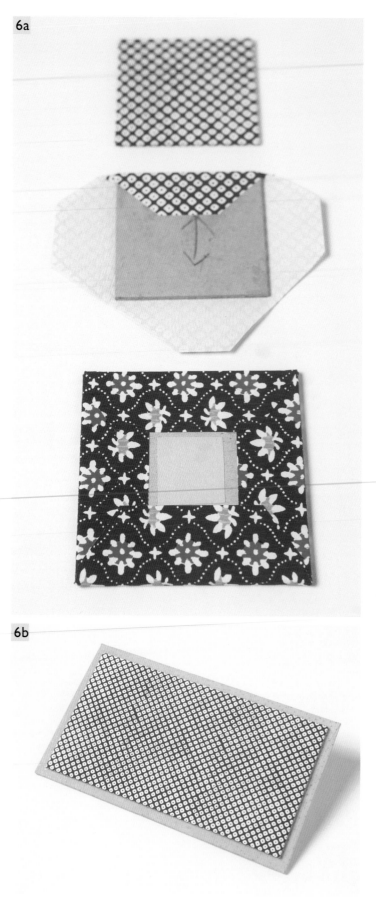

6a

6b

6 FINISH THE LID.

6a Cut, cover and glue together small pieces of board to create an interesting lid. Thread several buttons together to form a finial. Punch holes through all lid layers except for the liner, and sew on the finial. To protect the finial as the liner is being pressed onto the lid, arrange two stacks of small boards, side-by-side with a gap in between the size of the finial and its anchor boards. Invert the lid over this setup. Glue the lid liner with undiluted PVA, wipe off excess glue from the edges, and center this board on the lid. Hold this liner in place for a few minutes, until it stops sliding and begins to set. Place a pressing board and weights on top, and let sit for a half hour to one hour.

6b Glue the tray to the base platform. Apply undiluted PVA to the bottom of the tray. Wipe off excess glue from the edges. Center the tray on the platform and hold in place for a few minutes, until it begins to set. Invert the tray and place a pressing board and a heavy weight on top. Let sit for a half hour to one hour.

7 LINE THE BOX and attach the feet. If sewing buttons (feet) to the base platform, punch holes and sew on buttons before lining the box. If gluing buttons with either epoxy or wood glue, attach buttons after lining the box. Cut a piece of two-ply museum board just large enough to fit inside the tray, with a little breathing room. Cut a piece of covering paper:
Height = height of board, plus 1 1/2" (4 cm)
Width = width of board, plus 1 1/2" (4 cm)
Paste out the paper and center the board on it. Cut the corners and finish the edges (see The Basics, p.124). Press briefly. Glue the wrong side of this board with undiluted PVA, wipe away excess glue from its edges, and drop the liner into the tray. Hold for a few minutes until the glue begins to set. Put a scrap board (cut to fit) and weights in the tray, and let sit a half hour to one hour.

7

This is indeed a sweet container, and a versatile one as well. It can hold a single piece of chocolate or a ton of St. Valentine's Day cards. The Candy Box, like the prototypical Whitman's Sampler, consists of two nesting trays. Because this is a simple project—the second tray is an exact repeat of the first—it is a good candidate for multiples. To make an edition of three small boxes instead of one requires just a few more minutes in cutting time, an extra hour or two in construction time, and a couple of dollars more in materials. Be brave: produce an edition!

A survey of vintage candy boxes reveals yards of embossed, gilt, and lace papers. For my edition, I likewise selected a textured, brilliant red paper. The boxes are lined with antique tea chest paper—paper used in Japan to wrap bricks of tea.

the candy box...
memories of fudge and friendships

MATERIALS	Binder's board	Decorative paper
	Bristol or museum board	PVA, mixture and paste
	for linings	

getting started:
cutting the boards for the tray

- Cut out the boards for the inside tray, following the layout shown.
- Base:

  Height = desired height of box, plus two paper (covering) thicknesses

  Width = desired width of box, plus two paper (covering) thicknesses
- Head and tail walls:

  Width = desired width of box, plus two paper (covering) thicknesses

  Depth = desired depth of box, plus one board thickness, plus one lining thickness
- Spine and fore-edge walls:

  Height = height of base, plus two board thicknesses

  Depth = desired depth of box, plus one board thickness, plus one lining thickness

1a, b CONSTRUCT THE TRAY
(see The Basics, page 122). Smooth all
seams with a sanding stick.

1a

CUTTING LAYOUT FOR ONE BOX

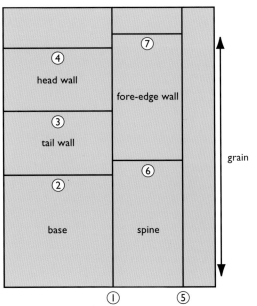

1b

CUTTING LAYOUT FOR THREE BOXES

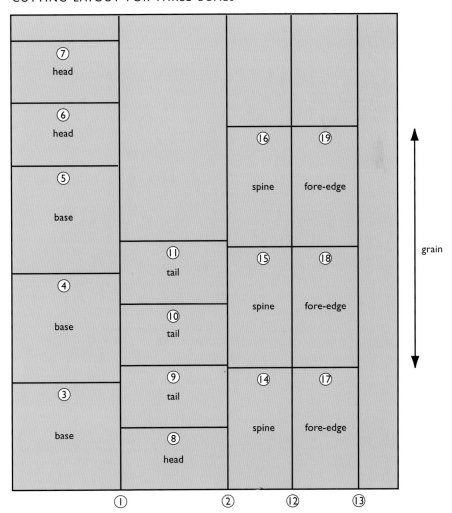

2a

2b

2a, b **COVER THE TRAY.** Cut out the covering paper—a strip twice the depth of the tray plus 1 1/2" (4 cm), and long enough to wrap around all four walls plus 1/2" (1 cm). If the paper is too short to wrap around the tray in one continuous strip, piece together two shorter strips, making sure that the seam falls on a corner of the tray. Cover the tray (see The Basics, page 123).

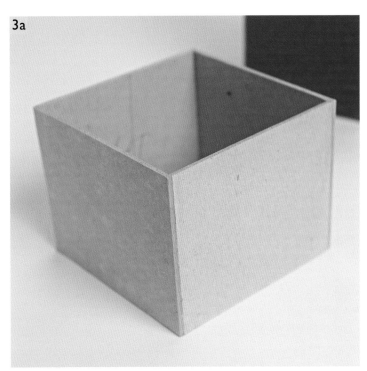

3a

3 **CUT OUT THE BOARDS** for the outside tray following the layout in Step 1. This tray is slightly larger than your inside tray.

3a To measure for its parts you must use your completed inside tray as a pattern. Place your tray on the squared corner of a piece of board (see page 118).

3b Make sure the grain runs from head to tail on both units, and that the spine and tail of the tray are flush with the squared
corner. Mark for cutting. Cut.
Base:
Height = height of tray plus two paper (covering) thicknesses
Width = width of tray plus two paper (covering) thicknesses
Head and tail walls:
Width = width of tray plus two paper (covering) thicknesses
Depth = depth of tray plus one board thickness
Spine and fore-edge walls:
Height = height of base plus two board thicknesses
Depth = depth of tray plus one board thickness

NEXT **CONSTRUCT AND COVER THE TRAY** (as in Steps 1 and 2).

NEXT **CUT OUT THE TWO PLAT-FORMS.** These boards are identical in size. They extend beyond the parameters of the larger tray by one board thickness in all four directions. Place the larger tray on the squared corner of a piece of board, flush spine and flush tail. Add two board thicknesses to the height and the width of the tray. This will later be redistributed as a one-board-thickness margin around all edges. Mark and cut out two boards.

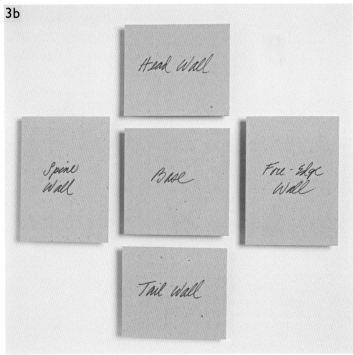

3b

Head Wall

Spine Wall

Base

Fore-Edge Wall

Tail Wall

4 COVER BOTH PLATFORMS.

Cut out two pieces of decorative paper, larger than the boards by 1¹/₂" (4 cm) in both height and width.

4a Make sure the grain runs from head to tail. Cover the boards, cut the corners and finish the edges (see The Basics, page 124).

4b Cut two pieces of scrap paper to fill in the remaining exposed board. This filler will balance the board, inducing it to flatten and to adhere more strongly to the tray.

NEXT **GLUE THE TRAYS** to the platforms. Brush undiluted PVA onto the bottom of the larger tray; wipe excess glue away from the edges. Center the tray on the wrong side of the lid platform. The other platform becomes the base platform. There should be a uniform small extension of a single board thickness beyond the edges of the tray. Hold these two units together for a few minutes, until the tray stops sliding and begins to stick. Flip the box over and place newsprint, a board, and a weight on top of the lid. Keep weighted until dry. Repeat all of these steps with the inside tray. Remember that this tray is smaller than the outside tray. When you are centering the tray on the base platform, the extension of the platform will be larger than one board thickness.

4a

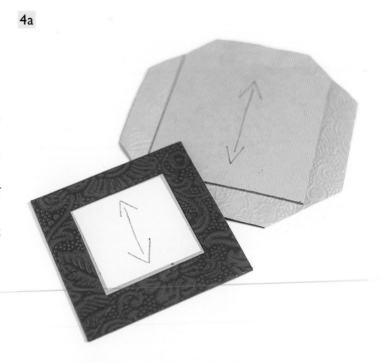

4b

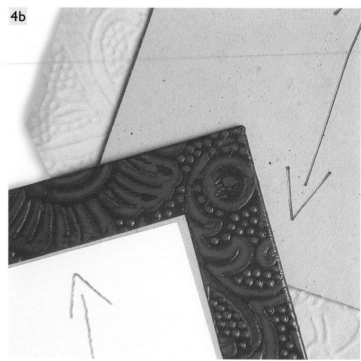

5a

5b

5 LINE THE TRAYS.

5a If lining the box with a medium or heavyweight paper, cut out two pieces of paper, one to fit inside of each tray. Don't forget to anticipate the stretch of the paper against the grain, and be sure to cut it a bit narrower in width.

5b Paste out these papers and stick them down. Press, as usual, with newsprint, a board, and a weight, until dry. (If your box is quite small, there is no need to press it.)

If lining the box with a delicate or lightweight paper (such as the gold paper pictured here), it is first necessary to card the paper around boards. Cut out two pieces of lightweight board (bristol or museum board) to the same dimensions:
Height = height of interior of small tray, minus $1/8$" (.3 cm)
Width = width of interior of small tray, minus $1/8$" (.3 cm)
Cut out 2 pieces of covering paper:
Height = height of boards, plus $1^1/2$" (4 cm)
Width = width of boards, plus $1^1/2$" (4 cm)
Cover the boards, cut the corners, and finish the edges. (see The Basics, page 124.)

Apply undiluted PVA to the backs of these boards, wipe away excess glue, and carefully lower the boards into the trays. Hold for a few minutes until the glue begins to set. Cut a piece of scrap board to fit inside each tray. Drop this board into the tray, place a weight on top, and press until dry.

To create a dazzling display of color and pattern, cover the individual parts of the box—trays, platforms, and liners—with a mix of papers.

*What is more tender than a ribbon-tied bundle of letters? Pushed to the back of a desk drawer or aban-
doned in a dark closet, they are poignant testimony to friendship and love. They deserve a box of their own.
Here, the letters nestle within a tray; the tray is tucked inside an extended case. The ribbons, besides being
decorative, restrain the letters and also allow their graceful removal from the depths of the tray. The box
closes, seemingly magically, with hidden magnets.*

*My choice of a textured cloth and a patterned lining paper is not accidental. Because it is difficult
to totally disguise the presence of magnets, lively materials help to distract the eye. The beautiful hand-
painted paste paper, made by Lost Link Design Studio, is based on techniques used in the production of
cover and endpapers in Europe from the late sixteenth through the eighteenth century. A wonderful book
on the subject, originally published in 1942 and still unsurpassed, is Rosamond B. Loring's Decorated
Book Papers (Harvard University Press).*

the letter box...
memories of lives past and present

MATERIALS			
	Bookcloth	Bristol or museum board	Magnetic strips
	Binder's board	Lining paper	PVA, mixture and paste
	(100 point)	Ribbon	

getting started:
cutting the boards for the tray

The goal is a snug fit, with just enough breathing room to allow the ribbons to lift the letters out of the box. To determine the height of the tray, find your tallest letter; to determine width, find your widest letter. Follow the formula below:

- Base:

  Height = height of tallest letter plus ⅛" (.3 cm)

  Width = width of widest letter plus ⅛" (.3 cm)

- Head and tail walls:

  Width = width of widest letter plus ⅛" (.3 cm)

  Depth = 1½" (4 cm) or desired depth

- Spine and fore-edge walls:

  Height = height of base board, plus two board thicknesses

  Depth = 1½" or desired depth, matched to head and tail walls

1a

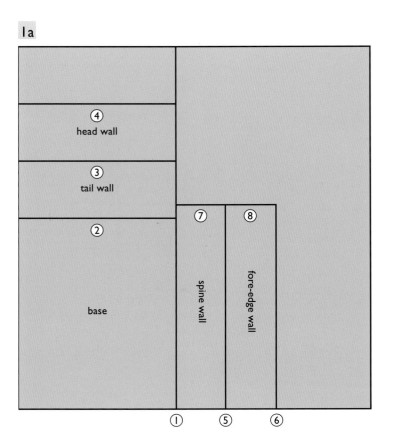

grain

1b

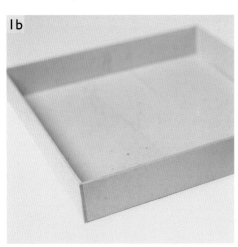

1a, b   CONSTRUCT THE TRAY
(see The Basics, page 122).

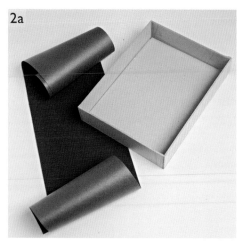

2a

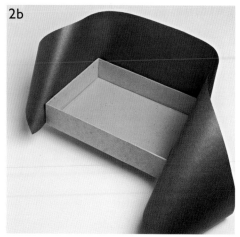

2b

2c

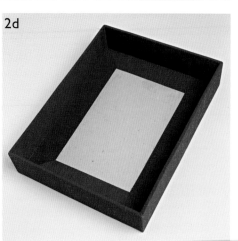

2d

2 COVER THE TRAY.

2a–c Cut out the covering cloth—a strip twice the depth of the tray plus 1 1/2" (4 cm), and long enough to wrap around all four walls plus 1/2" (1 cm). If the cloth is too short to wrap around the tray in one continuous strip, then piece together two shorter strips, making sure that the seam falls on a corner of the tray.

2d **Cover the tray** (see The Basics, page 22).

3

space = 2 board thicknesses

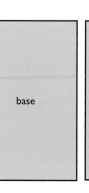

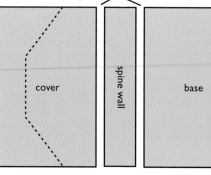
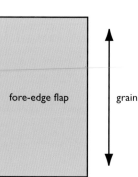

cover   spine wall   base   fore-edge wall   fore-edge flap   grain

3 CUT THE BOARDS FOR THE CASE.
Select boards thick enough to accommodate the magnetic strips that will be embedded in the cover and the fore-edge flap (Minimum board thickness: 100 point).

The height is the same for all five case boards:
Height = height of the covered tray, plus two board thicknesses
The width of the boards is the same for the three main panels:

Base = width of tray
Fore-edge flap = width of tray
Cover = width of tray (to be adjusted)
The depth of the walls is as follows:
Fore-edge wall = depth of covered tray, plus a hair
Spine wall = depth of fore-edge wall, plus one board thickness
From your scrap board, cut a slender strip two board thicknesses in width. This will be a joint spacer. See above for a diagram of the board layout.

4

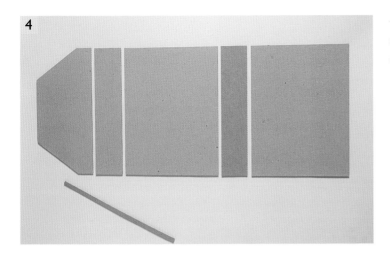

4   **TRIM AND ANGLE** the cover board, as desired. Smooth all sharp edges and corners with a sanding stick.

5a   **APPLY THE MAGNETIC STRIPS.** Draw a pencil line ³/₄" (2 cm) away from the angled edge of the cover. Draw a parallel line ¹/₂" (1 cm), or the width of your magnet, away from the first line. Cut two magnetic strips to the length of these lines.

5b   Cut and peel up a layer of board equal to the thickness of the magnet.

5c   Remove the backing paper and sink the magnet into this recessed area. Find the corresponding area on the fore-edge flap for the placement of the second magnet. Be precise because the magnet will not hold unless the two are perfectly aligned.

5d   Cut and peel away board. Sink the magnet.

5a

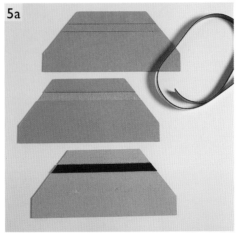

5b

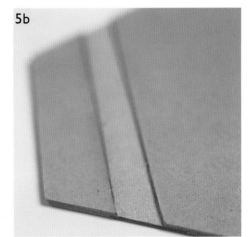

5c

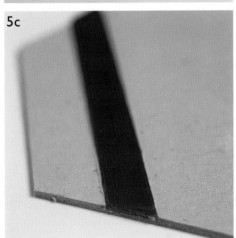

5d

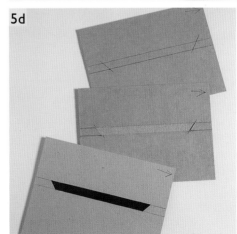

6a

6b

6c

NEXT   CUT THE CLOTH FOR THE CASE:

Height = height of boards plus 1 1/2" (4 cm) for turn-ins

Width = width of boards laid out, plus joint spacing plus 1 1/2" (4 cm) for turn-ins

NEXT   CONSTRUCT THE CASE.

Note: When gluing up the case, the cover board is glued magnet side *up* on the cloth; the fore-edge flap is glued magnet side *down*. Glue the boards and apply them to the cloth, working from left to right and using the joint spacer between every two boards. Flip the case over and press down well, eliminating any air bubbles.

NEXT   CUT THE CORNERS and finish the edges (see The Basics, page 122). As with The Patchwork Box, when dealing with the angled panel you will need to invent a pattern of cuts that allows for the clean coverage of all corners.

6a   COVER THE (INSIDE) WALLS.
Cut two strips of cloth from your leftovers to cover the walls, fill in the joints, and extend onto the three main panels:
Height = height of case minus two board thicknesses
Width = depth of spine wall plus 1 3/4" (4.5 cm)
Make sure, as always, that the grain runs from head to tail.

6b, c   Glue out one strip and position it, centered, on the spine wall. Press it down quickly and work the cloth into the two joints with the edge of your bone folder, moving back and forth between the two joints until the fabric has stuck. Press the cloth onto the cover and base panels. Repeat with the fore-edge wall.

7

7   LINE THE CASE. Cut two pieces of paper to line the cover and the fore-edge flap:
Height = height of case minus two board thicknesses
Width = width of cover and fore-edge flap, minus two board thicknesses
Remember to anticipate the stretch of the pasted or glued paper in width, and cut accordingly. Glue or paste these papers to adhere them. Put newsprint, boards, and weights on these two panels, and let dry.

NEXT   GLUE THE TRAY TO THE CASE. Cut two pieces of scrap cloth, large enough to fill in (1) the bottom (outside) of the tray; and (2) the base board of the case. Glue them out and stick them down. Using undiluted PVA, paint a thin, consistent layer of glue onto the bottom of the tray. Wipe excess glue from the edges. Position the tray on the base of the case, centered head to tail, and hold until the glue begins to set. Fill with weights, and let dry.

8a

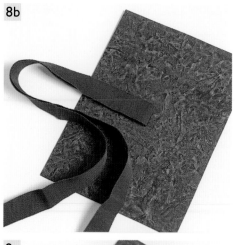

8b

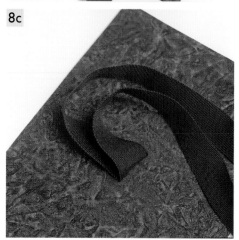

8c

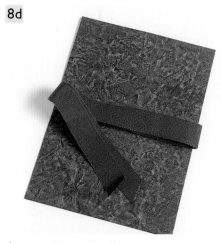

8d

8 ATTACH RIBBONS AND LINE THE TRAY.

8a, b Cut a piece of lightweight board to fit inside of the tray. Allow ¹⁄₈" (.3 cm) breathing room in both height and width. To cover this board, cut a piece of either paper or cloth to the following dimensions:

Height = height of board plus 1¹⁄₂" (4 cm)
Width = width of board plus 1¹⁄₂" (4 cm)
Adhere the covering material to the board, cut the corners, and finish the edges (see The Basics, page 20). Fill in the back of the board with scrap paper. Select a chisel the width of your ribbons and make a vertical slit through the center of this board.

8c, d Push the ends of two ribbons through the slit and glue down with undiluted PVA on the back of the board. Paint a thin layer of undiluted PVA on this board, wipe off excess glue from the edges, and carefully lower the board into the tray. Keep the ribbons away from the glue. Put a protective waste sheet on top of this liner, fill the tray with boards and a weight, and let dry.

NEXT **GLUE THE CASE WALLS TO THE TRAY.** Brush a thin layer of undiluted PVA onto the spine wall of the tray. Wipe excess glue from the edges. Roll the tray onto its spine wall; fill the tray with weights and press until the spine walls of the tray and case are thoroughly bonded. Repeat with fore-edge wall.

Tip: *To Line the Tray with a Framed Photo*

Remove the letters from the box and discover an image of the writer—or the recipient—framed beneath. Alter the previous instructions in two places: (1) In cutting out the boards for the tray (Step 1), increase the depth of the walls to accommodate the additional thicknesses of the covered mat and the photograph; and (2) replace Step 12 with the following:

1. Cut two pieces of lightweight board to fit inside the tray. Allow $1/8$" (.3 cm) breathing room in height and width.

2. Cut a window out of one of the boards. Cut a piece of decorative paper, to cover this mat, to the following dimensions:
Height = height of board plus $1 1/2$" (4 cm)
Width = width of board plus $1 1/2$" (4 cm)

3. Cover the mat, by pasting out the paper and centering the board on the paper. Finish the interior of the mat only (see The Picture Frame Box, Step 2, page 127). Do not cut corners or finish the outer edges.

4. Glue the two ribbons onto the back of the mat.

5. Affix the photo, with pressure-sensitive adhesive, in the proper location on the second (uncut) board.

6. Glue the wrong side of the mat with undiluted PVA to the photo board. Keep the ribbons free of glue. Press.

7. Place the mat, wrong side up, on the workbench. Cut the corners of the paper, staying $1 1/2$ board thicknesses away from the tip of the board. Remember that your "board" consists of the mat, the photo, and the photo board. Re-apply paste to the turn-ins, and adhere them. Fill in the back of the board with scrap paper.

8. Glue the board to the tray by painting a thin layer of undiluted PVA on the board, wiping off excess glue from the edges, and carefully lowering the board into the tray. Put a protective waste sheet on top of the liner, fill the tray with boards and a weight, and let dry.

If you wish to protect the photograph, cut a piece of Plexiglas to the height and width of the two boards, and sandwich it between the mat and the photo board before completing the turn-ins (Step 7).

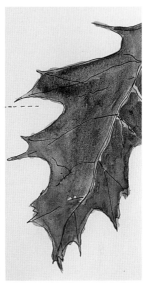

Materials List

JOURNALING SUPPLIES Every journaler uses, at minimum, a blank book and a pen or pencil. Some journalers have favorite fountain pens or particular styles of books they like to use. Or they make their own one-of–a-kind books, such as those described and show-cased in later chapters. Many other supplies are useful for creating and designing journals. Keeping a journal box is a creative way to store and personalize your own journal-keeping materials.

BOOKBINDING SUPPLIES Certain tools and materials are required to hand-bind books. Some of the materials listed here can be replaced by others—you can, for example, make your own book cloth—but it's a good idea to have a sturdy glue brush, a bone folder, and appropriate adhesives on hand (especially PVA glue, a bookbinding glue) when making books.

ART MATERIALS AND SUPPLIES Nowadays you can purchase many different craft materials and art supplies at nationally franchised art and craft superstores. The resources section in the back of the book also lists Internet and mail-order

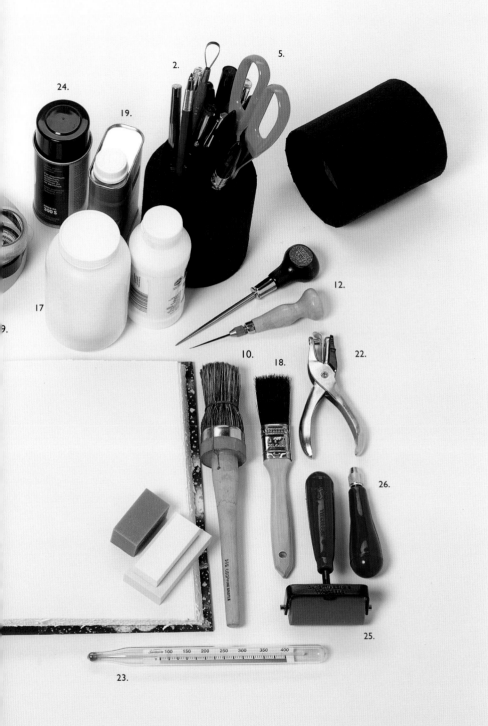

◀ 1. blank book ballpoint, fountain, or dip pens

2. inks pencils, erasers, markers, crayons

3. spray adhesive, glue stick, or PVA glue

4. tape   5. scissors   6. binder's tape   7. bone

folder 8. matte knife   9. ruler   10. glue brush

11. needle and thread   12. awl   13. screw posts

14. clasps 15. beads 16. leather lacing 17. gesso

18. paint brush   19. xylene and other solvents

20. respirator or dust mask   21. spackle and

knife 22. hole punch or drill   23. candy ther-

mometer   24. spray enamel   25. brayer

26. carving tools   27. sand paper or sanding block

supply companies, from which you can
buy artists' materials such as those listed
here and throughout the book.

OTHER TOOLS, SUPPLIES, AND MATE-
RIALS The tools and materials listed
here, some of which you may already have
in your home or studio, are used in many
of the projects in the book. Be sure to
read and follow any manufacturer's warnings before using chemicals such as solvents and adhesives.

Blank Books

A blank book is the starting point for just about every journal showcased in this book. On the right are unused blank books, ranging from one-of-a-kind, leather-covered, hand-bound journals, to store-bought, spiral-bound notebooks and just about every variation in between. The recent revival of diary-writing and journal-keeping has created a market for journals, which are now available just about everywhere, from your local arts supply store to stationery boutiques, craft fairs, and even your corner drugstore. Many of the blank books shown here are created by the same artists whose work is featured throughout the rest of this book.

Historical Journals

A rich history of personal, hand-written diaries begins with the earliest known manuscript dairy, the *Kagero Diary*, written by a Japanese woman in the tenth century, to well-known published diaries such as *The Diary of Anne Frank* and the diaries of Anaïs Nin. Visual journals are similar to diaries in that they're confessional and personal, but they also contain more than daily written entries. Your local bookstore sells fully reprinted visual journals, such as *Spilling Open: The Art of Becoming Yourself* by Sabrina Ward Harrison and *The Journey Is the Destination: The Journals of Dan Eldon*. These are facsimile journals—actual reprints—containing exquisitely embellished journal pages similar to the journals featured in this book.

The history of visual journals is not well documented, but collectors of diaries and historical journals are aware of books with unusual contents that date to the mid-1800s, when the first diaries filled with more than written entries began to appear. Here is a small gallery containing examples of these visual diaries of historical note that are the pre-decessors to current journal keepers' books.

ABOVE, AND FACING PAGE, TOP: From the collection of Sally Mac Namara-Ivey & Kevin Ivey. FACING PAGE, BOTTOM: Handwritten account of a woman's trip to Europe in the summer of 1897, which discusses life aboard the Ocean Liners "La Champagne" and the "Kaiser Wilhelm" as well as travels in Europe. From the collection of Sally Mac Namara-Ivey & Kevin Ivey.

BELOW: One of "Self-Taught" artist James Castle's journals circa 1930's, "BLAW Book" challenges the concept of the codex format and contains stylized rendered scenes and illustrations. Courtesy of a private collector. RIGHT: A young woman's hand-written diary and scrapbook of her trip from Longport to Chicago's Worlds Fair including a visit to Niagara Falls and the city of Chicago. From the collection of Sally Mac Namara-Ivey & Kevin Ivey. BOTTOM: A diary kept by Alice Bentley onboard the ship "Normandie" which begins in New York City and ends in LeHavre with photos and mementos. From the collection of Sally Mac Namara-Ivey & Kevin Ivey

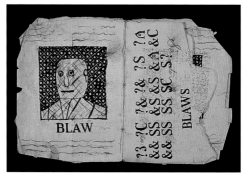

LEFT: 200 handwritten pages from a record book with partial diary entries dating from the 1790's. Includes an interesting entry about General George Washington's death. From the collection of Sally Mac Namara-Ivey & Kevin Ivey. BELOW: This book contains over 100 personal and business letters received by a young man just graduated from Yale University who spends his summer sketching and trying to sell his sketches. From the collection of Sally Mac Namara-Ivey & Kevin Ivey.

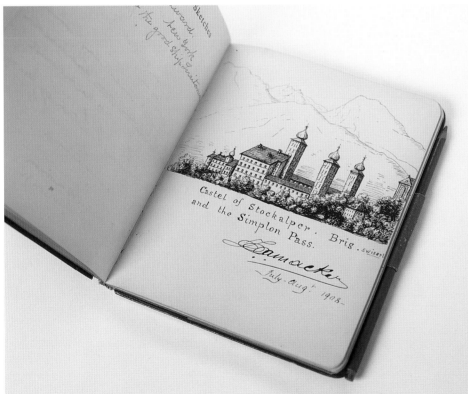

ABOVE: Contains an account of a trip to England and other parts of Europe on board the ship "Lusitania" with records of places visited including lunch with Lord and Lady Furness. From the collection of Sally Mac Namara-Ivey & Kevin Ivey. MIDDLE RIGHT: This book contains ten handwritten autographed poetry pieces dating from 1845–1848, each with braided hair pieces of each author. From the collection of Sally Mac Namara-Ivey & Kevin Ivey. BOTTOM RIGHT: "Nellies Ledger" Created from a ledger belonging to the sister of Self-Taught artist James Castle. Narratives and patterns are created by collages of found illustrations pasted on pages covered with a wash of soot and saliva ink. Courtesy Private Collector.

Making Your Own Journals

So you want to keep a journal. Many wonderful blank journals are available from your local stationery, gift, and arts and crafts stores. Bookbinders also sometimes sell blank books to small local shops in the communities where they live and work. Visit a university bookstore or independent bookseller near you to find small-run, individually created blank books. You may also look at arts and crafts shows—anywhere bookbinders might sell their work.

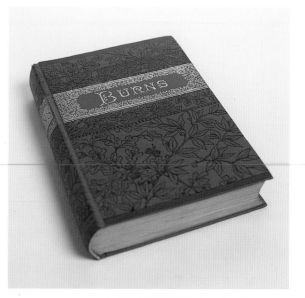

But if you're ready to make your own journal, here are three examples of simple books you can create without much experience or bookbinding skills. In addition, an extensive bibliography at the end of this book offers recommendations for detailed bookbinding tutorial publications.

Creating a Spiral-Bound Book

MATERIALS

writing paper

decorative paper

other ephemera
such as envelopes,
handmade paper,
printed pages,
mailing and label
tags, photographs,
post cards, etc.

To create your own personal journal, let's start with a very simple technique that requires no bookbinding experience or special knowledge. Many journalers write and create in spiral-bound journals, as seen throughout this book, instead of case-bound journals for two reasons: They can lay the journal flat without stressing its spine, and the spiral binding allows items to be added within their pages without the book "yawning" open when it is closed. Creating your own spiral-bound book can actually be less expensive than buying one in the store. But most importantly, creating your own allows you the freedom to add unique elements such as printed pages, envelopes, decorative papers, and different colored sheets into the binding.

ONE

STEP ONE GATHER AND COLLATE YOUR PAGES Gather the pages and other items you plan to have bound into your new book and collate them into the correct order. You can use a binder clip to hold the pages together until just prior to binding. Most service bureaus can fit up to an inch of material in their spiral-binding machines and can even accept heavy card stock or bookbinding board for the front and back covers.

TWO

STEP TWO SPIRAL-BIND YOUR BOOK You will need to locate a service bureau that has the equipment necessary to spiral-bind books and booklets. Most local copy centers have this equipment, and many service bureaus will create your book while you wait. From start to finish, your book can be created in an afternoon!

Rebinding a Store-Bought Journal

MATERIALS

drawing paper

needle

thread

ONE

TWO

Maybe you've already found a style of journal that you like, but it isn't exactly what you need for every occasion. Maybe you like to use watercolors on some pages, and pens and pencils on others. Wouldn't it be great to have a book that had watercolor paper on some pages, and lined or unlined writing paper on others? With this simple re-binding technique, you can deconstruct a single-signature binding to create a book for all occasions. In order to rebind a store-bought book as described in these steps, you'll need a one-signature book, also known as a pamphlet. A signature is a group of pages that are folded in half and sewn along the fold to hold the pages together. One-signature journals contain only one group of pages sewn together in the middle. You can sometimes find these types of books stapled instead of sewn. Either type of book will work for this project.

STEP ONE **DISASSEMBLE THE PAGES** Remove the thread or staples that hold the book together. The holes in the fold of the pages will be used when re-sewing the pages back together. Add new pages, such as colored sheets, printed pages from a computer, or thicker paper for drawing, to the signature of old pages.

STEP TWO **REBIND THE PAGES** When the new pages have been added into the signature, use a needle to punch holes through these new sheets to correspond to the rest of the holes in the original signature. Sew your reconstructed signature and the original cover, if there was one, together with a needle and thread. Tightly tie the ends of the thread together inside the signature in the middle of the book, and you're ready to write!

Rebinding a Vintage Book

MATERIALS

writing paper

decorative paper

razor

PVA glue

glue brush

damp rag

sandpaper

This is the most difficult of the three projects, but it's also the most fun! With this simple technique, you can bind your own individual blank book with any vintage book cover of your choice.

STEP ONE GATHER THE MATERIALS
Begin by locating a hardcover book with an interesting cover. Try used book stores, library book sales, and flea markets. Next, gather your new pages. Experiment with different writing papers, as some types of papers are opaque, while others are transparent; some papers are durable enough to take artists' materials, some are best used for writing only. It may be a good idea to attempt this project with a book that is smaller than 8.5" x 11" (22cm x 28cm), a standard-size sheet of writing paper, so you will be able to find paper readily from retail paper vendors and copy centers.

STEP TWO DISASSEMBLE THE BOOK
Carefully remove the book block—all the pages inside the book—from the cover by slicing along the folds between the book block and the cover, being careful not to cut the cover. You should have two items when you're finished, the book block and the cover, which consists of the front cover, the spine, and the back cover. Here's a tip: Some books have spines that are glued to the book block and thus are not appropriate for this project. If you can look down through the spine from the top of the book when it's held open, you've got the right kind of binding. Professional bookbinders will completely remove the endsheets (the heavy paper glued to the inside of the covers) before rebinding a book. If you're not comfortable disassembling the covers entirely, simply use sandpaper to smooth any frayed ends or loose glue along the cover's inside edges.

THREE

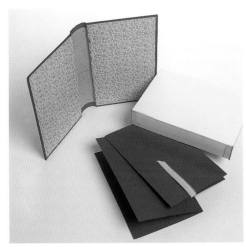

FOUR

STEP THREE   **CREATE A NEW BOOK BLOCK**   Carefully measure the removed book block and write down its thickness, length, and width. Once you have decided on a type of paper for the pages of your book, assemble as many sheets as it takes to create a stack that is as thick as your original vintage book. Take this stack and the book's measurements to your service bureau and ask them to perfect-bind your sheets—glue the sheets together along one edge to create a new spine—and cut them down to the exact size as the old book block. When it is done, you will have a new book block the same size as the one you removed but containing blank pages.

STEP FOUR   **REBIND THE BOOK**   Here's the fun part! Gather two thick sheets of paper to be used as your endsheets. Your new endsheets should be the same length as your new book block but twice as wide. When these sheets are folded in half, they should be the same width and length as your book block. Place a strip of a PVA-type glue approximately one inch wide along the folded edges of the new end-sheets, and glue them to the book block so that the folds of the endsheets are adjacent to the spine. Next, carefully cover the entire outer side of the endsheet with glue and press the new book block into the old cov-ers. Remove any stray glue with a damp rag. As most of us don't have a book press handy, you can stack a pile of books or something heavy such as bricks on top of your newly glued book. Allow it to dry overnight.

Daily Journals

MATERIALS

writing pages

decorative paper

awl

needle

thread

beads (optional)

Daily journals are the most common and flexible journals. Daily journals contain diary entries, wisdom, everyday minutia, and ephemera collected from daily life such as ticket stubs, labels, stickers, business cards, and photographs. There are as many formats of daily journals as there are journalers, but there are a few common elements, such as pictures of pets and the ubiquitous coffee-cup ring. Artist Wendy Hale Davis keeps beautiful daily journals, and, being a professional bookbinder, she even binds her own exquisite, leatherbound books. They contain daily entries, Wendy's beautiful handwritten calligraphic headings, and items and objects glued onto the pages.

I STARTED KEEPING JOURNALS IN 1970 BECAUSE MY BOYFRIEND AT THE TIME DID. OVER TIME MY BOOKS HAVE BECOME MORE INTENTIONAL AND ARTISTIC.

Artist: Wendy Hale Davis

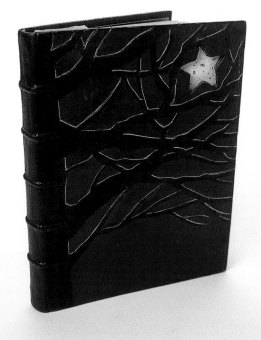

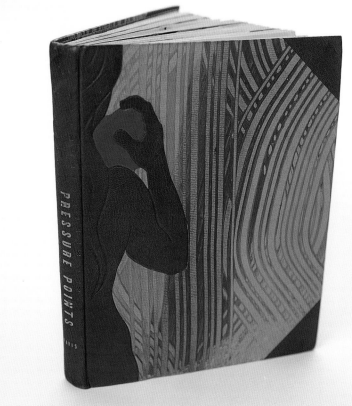

Step by Step:

ONE

TWO

THREE

STEP ONE FOLD THE SIGNATURE AND COVER MATERIAL A one-signature book is a very easy way to begin making your own books. Begin by folding four or five writing pages in half to form a single signature. Then fold decorative paper in half to make the cover.

STEP TWO SEW THE SINGLE SIGNATURE Use an awl to pre-punch holes into the crease or spine of your book. We have pre-punched five holes in our example and used embroidery floss that we have coated with beeswax to prevent knotting. Begin sewing through the spine from the top and outside of the book down through to the bottom hole, then sew back up again to the top hole. Tie the two loose ends together tightly.

STEP THREE EMBELLISH WITH BEADS Tie beads onto the loose ends of the thread for a decorative element.

notes:

Make your daily journal out of sturdy material. It will be used quite a bit.

To prompt yourself to create and write something in your journal on a regular basis, date the pages.

Use your daily journal as a place to work out ideas for themed books, such as garden or recipe journals.

After many, many years have passed, long after you're gone, your journals will be read by friends or family members. Think about writing down the personal stories from your life that only you will remember. Think of all the times you say to someone, "I remember back when ... " and transcribe these stories into your journal. They will be priceless to the people who come after you.

TOP LEFT AND BOTTOM RIGHT: This journal was collaged by Dorothy Krause with materials collected on a two week trip to Vietnam. BOTTOM LEFT: Judy Serebrin kept this journal in Cambridge, England, to earn credits for a master of fine arts degree.
TOP RIGHT: Dorothy Krause remembers a year she taught at the Massachusetts College of Art in Boston with this book.

TOP LEFT: Kez van Oudheusden's visual journal of an academic semester. LEFT AND TOP RIGHT: Two books by Marilyn Reaves. ABOVE: Roz Stendahl's "Things to Do Until I See You Again."

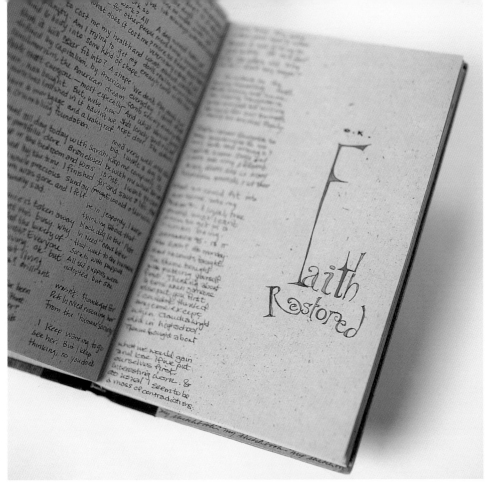

ABOVE: A daily journal by Judy Serebrin.

RIGHT: Judy Serebrin's "Israel Journal I."

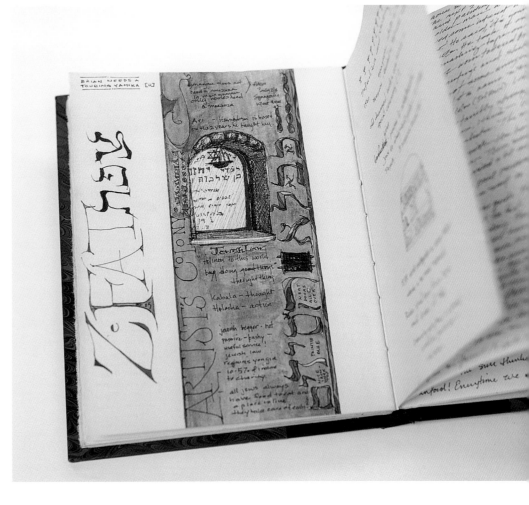

Travel Journals

MATERIALS

pen

pencil

watercolors

paint brush

glue stick

tape

kneaded eraser

razor

**a Swiss army knife
and a flashlight may
also come in handy**

Travel journals are probably the most inspirational way to keep a visual journal. We all want to remember our memories of visiting new places and meeting new people. Keeping a journal while you are travelling and while your experiences are still fresh in your mind seems to be a natural thing to do. Bruce Kremer has been keeping travel journals for twenty years, filling over a dozen of them in that time. Travel journals often contain common elements, and we will discuss three of them in detail.

MY TRAVEL JOURNAL CONTAINS WRITTEN ENTRIES,

COLLAGES, AND DAILY OCCURRENCES.

Artist: Bruce Kremer

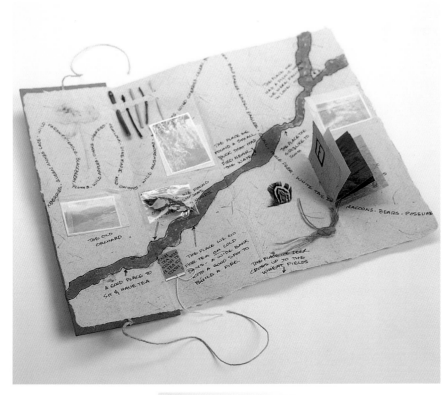

TOP LEFT: Elizabeth Clark deconstructed a childhood geography book and reassembled it, including etchings, photocopied images and handmade paper. TOP RIGHT, BOTTOM LEFT AND RIGHT: Artist: Bruce Kremer

Step by Step:

ONE

TWO

THREE

ABOVE LEFT: This book is filled with ephemera and scraps recording events which Bruce Kremer has incorporated with written entries to remember his journey. ABOVE RIGHT: The pages of Bruce Kremer's travel journals embody places visited and people met through collected and layered mementos and the written word. LEFT: This book records Bruce Kremer's around-the-world trip taken in 1991 and features written entries and found ephemera and mementos attached to the page. FACING PAGE, TOP: While traveling in Morocco, Evelyn Eller remembered buying an old Koran in Istanbul and thought that the pages from that book would make an ideal background for this travel journal. FACING PAGE, MIDDLE: Cheryl Slyter created this journal after a trip to Spain and France in April, 1999. She bound photos printed on Arches Test Wove paper as the, "…tactile quality of the paper is delightful." FACING PAGE, BOTTOM LEFT AND RIGHT: This book was created to be both a reference and notebook/sketchbook for Laura Blacklow's visit to Dallas. Each board is covered with half of the inner city map.

STEP ONE **COLLECT PAPER ITEMS AND OTHER EPHEMERA** Be sure to collect paper ephemera that can be added to your journal, such as postage stamps, local wine and beer labels, ticket stubs, currency, cigarette packs, candy wrappers, receipts, and especially handwritten notes, directions, or letters in local script. Keep your glue stick, knife, or tape handy.

STEP TWO **PLOT AND RECORD YOUR PROGRESS** Look for local maps, which can make great backgrounds for journal pages. You can also plot your progress with comments and memories of your own experiences right on the maps.

STEP THREE **NO CAMERA? DRAW IT!** Probably the most common element found in travel journals is photographs. But if you didn't bring a camera with you, a drawing is the next best thing. Use colored pencils, crayons, and even ballpoint pens to sketch what's around you.

A journal is a blank book just waiting for your creative input. It can be kept as memento of a place, time, or event. Here are examples of journals with different themes that can be used to facilitate writing:

GARDEN JOURNAL Document daily memories from tending or creating gardens

DREAM JOURNAL Record nightly dreams

TRAVEL JOURNAL Chronicle your travels

BABY JOURNAL Start during pregnancy, and continue after the birth of a new baby

WEDDING JOURNAL Document the time from an engagement to a wedding

ANNIVERSARY JOURNAL Record special recurring events

FAMILY JOURNAL Remember your family for the next generation with pictures and anecdotes

WINE JOURNAL Keep track of the wine you drink, and include the labels

READING JOURNAL Write about the books you've read

QUILTING JOURNAL Catalog family quilts, and include fabric swatches and pictures

ACTIVITY JOURNAL Describe a favorite hobby or sport

DAILY JOURNAL Document your daily life with words and pictures

RECIPE JOURNAL Keep a list of personal recipes, and include pictures of food, meals, and friends

notes:

Ask customs officials or local postal employees to stamp your journal.

If something you want to include is too heavy or too thick, use a blender pen to transfer a photocopy of it.

Save leaves and flowers to press into your journal. Make leaf impressions or use clear tape to completely tape in a flower.

Recipe Journals

MATERIALS

**card stock or
watercolor paper**

decorative paper

ribbon

needle

hole punch or drill

glue

scissors

photocorners

Simply put, a recipe journal is a book that contains recipes. But along with simple cooking instructions, a recipe journal may also document the cooking process, contain pictures of meals with friends, and include food labels and comments about favorite recipes. By personalizing a journal with handwritten notes, instructions, and comments, a recipe journal can become a family heirloom. Artist Anne Woods created a recipe journal to remember meals shared with good neighbors before moving across country. She shares not only her recipes but her thoughts, impressions, photographs, and drawings of her neighbors in this one-of-a-kind book.

I CREATED THIS JOURNAL FOR MY NEIGHBOURS AND
GOOD FRIENDS, TO COMMEMORATE RECIPES AND MEALS
WE HAVE SHARED TOGETHER.

Artist: Anne Woods

Artist: Anne Woods

Step by Step:

ONE

TWO

THREE

STEP ONE **GATHER THE MATERIALS** Pre-cut the card stock or watercolor paper to a uniform size. Gather your pictures, recipes, decorative papers, and other elements to include in your recipe journal.

STEP TWO **CREATE THE PAGES** Create your pages as individual pieces. Glue recipes to the pre-cut cardstock or watercolor paper, attach pictures of meals or wine labels, record your thoughts about meals with good friends, and even jot personal notes and hints about certain recipes. Each piece of cardstock should be a two-sided page, with elements on both the front and back. As each page is a single piece, experiment with laying them out in different orders before you bind them in. And remember to leave room at the edges of your pages for the holes and ribbon!

STEP THREE **BIND THE PAGES TOGETHER** Create a front and back cover with card-stock or watercolor paper. At the same spot on each of the cards, punch or drill two large holes. Slip a ribbon-threaded needle through each hole and tie with a decorative bow.

When writing in your journal, don't forget to write about the people around you, your family and friends. You may think now that a short visit by a distant relative isn't something to write about, but a hundred years from now, your future relatives may think differently. Think about what you would find interesting if you could read your great-grandmother or grandfathers journals. What was a typical day like? It may seem trite, but what does a loaf of bread cost? A first-class stamp? Why not place a first-class stamp into your journal? Take a picture of your home or your family, date your entries, and be sure to write somewhere in the front of your journal, "This book belongs to ..." with a date and, if possible, a picture of yourself.

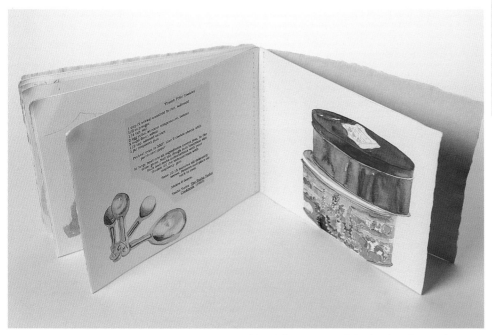

Katy Gilmore created this book to honor the everyday. It contains embellished, meaningful quotes; journal writing; and everyday observations.

notes:

Transcribe recipes from older family members. You may be surprised to know what goes into Grandma's meatloaf!

Take pictures of meals to remember good food and good friends.

Save interesting wine and food labels.

Garden Journals

MATERIALS

writing pages

decorative paper cover

hole punch or drill

screw posts

ribbon

leaves

inks

rubber stamps

decorative paper card
(optional)

A garden journal is a book kept to record the daily memories of tending or creating a garden. It contains entries such as a layout of your garden; actual plant material such as leaves, petals, or seeds; daily or weekly entries as to the progress of your garden; and tips, ideas, or wisdom gained from tending gardens. Artist Sherri Keisel created her journal, "A Gardner Reflects," after she had collected items from her gardening experience, but it's just as easy to create the book beforehand and add entries as you're inspired. The type of journal Sherri uses is perfect for a garden journal, which can become soiled from the wear and tear of working and writing in a garden. It is also expandable, which is a great feature for adding gardening mementos to the pages without making the book "yawn" when it is filled.

I WANTED TO CAPTURE THE CYCLE OF SEASONS AND THE DEPTH OF TEXTURES OF NATURE ENCOUNTERED IN A GARDENER'S LIFE THROUGH COLOR, TEXT AND ILLUSTRATION.

Artist: Sherri Keisel

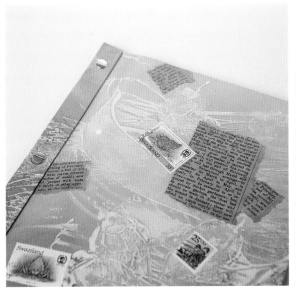

THIS PAGE: Sherri Keisel wanted to capture, with color, text and illustration, the cycle of seasons and the depth of textures in the surrounding nature encountered in a gardener's life.

Step by Step:

CREATING A DURABLE, SCREW-POST GARDEN JOURNAL

ONE

TWO

THREE

STEP ONE **ASSEMBLE YOUR MATERIALS**
Collect your pages, cover material, and
any other items you wish to bind into
your book. In this example, we're using a
hand-made, decorative heavyweight writing
paper for the cover.

STEP TWO **CREATE THE COVER**   In
our example, we've attached a decorative
card with a leaf impression onto the cover
and used a rubber-stamp alphabet set to
write "Garden Journal."

STEP THREE **BIND THE BOOK!**   When
the covers are designed, use either a hole
punch or a drill to create holes in the
binding for the screw posts. To finish the
book off, weave ribbon through the spine
so the book can be hung from a peg or
nail in a garden shed or greenhouse.

notes:

Bind envelopes into the book to
hold seeds of favorite plants.

Create a very personalized decorative
cover for your garden journal by
making your own paper, adding leaves
and petals you have saved from your
garden to the pulp.

Screw posts come in different colors
and patinas, so investigate the possibilities and choose one that's best for
you. For a more industrial look, you
can also use a machine bolt and nut.

The inspiration for Janis Cheek's "Gail's Garden" journal was her best friend's beautiful flower garden and how it changed throughout the summer and fall.

You may find keeping a journal to be a singular experience. Some people find that the most inspiring reason to keep a journal is to share them with others. You might enjoy hearing what friends think about the pages you've created, and you might be surprised by what they like or don't comment about. To gather inspiration from fellow journalers, find out where they get together, or form your own group. The Internet is a wonderful resource for bringing like-minded people together. When you discover communities of other journalers who share the same passions as you do, you might find yourself creating more often. The next time you write or create in your journal, remember that at any given time there are thousands of people all over the world also sitting down to their own personal journals.

Artists' Sketchbooks

MATERIALS

heavyweight pages

hole punch or drill

metal ring clasps

leather laces

beads

needle

thread (optional)

Artists' sketchbooks have existed for a long time. It may be fair to say that they are the true precursor to both diaries and journals. Early examples are Leonardo Da Vinci's "Codex Leicester" notebooks, dating from the early sixteenth century. His sketchbooks document the artist's process of creation in a way his finished works never could. Similarly, twentieth-century artists such as Tracy Moore use sketchbooks as a venue to create their own ideas in an intimate format, unencumbered by criticism. Tracey's journals contain ideas, bits of inspiration, and unfinished art as well as comments and narratives.

I USUALLY KEEP A JOURNAL OF THIS SIZE AS WELL AS A SMALL ONE THAT FITS IN MY POCKET FOR WHEN I AM UNABLE TO BRING MY LARGER JOURNAL ALONG. THEY ARE WHAT KEEP ME SANE, AS I DUMP MY INSANITY INTO THEM. THEY OPEN A DOORWAY TO A PLACE WHERE I CAN PLAY, WRITE, SKETCH, AND EVEN SOCIALIZE WITH OTHERS, COMPLETELY WITHOUT RULES.

Artist: Tracy Moore

The Journal of Tracy Moore.
Artist: Tracy Moore

Step by Step:

ONE

TWO

THREE

STEP ONE **GATHER THE MATERIALS** In this example, we will describe how to make a landscape-format book—one that is wider than it is tall—though your sketchbook can be any size you like. Be sure your pages are of uniform size and that your hole-punching tool can create holes in your pages large enough for the rings to fit through, but small enough so the rings don't slip, making the book unstable. You can find rings like the ones used here in local art- or craft-supply stores, or from the vendors listed in the back of the book.

STEP TWO **CREATE THE COVER** Be sure the hole punch can accommodate the cover material, which is thicker than the pages. In this example, we have chosen artists' canvas that is sturdy enough for our use. On the front cover, we have attached a large bead and coin to serve as a clasp to hold the book shut. Simply pre-punch small holes with an awl through the cover where you plan to place the clasp, and then sew the bead or coin in place with strong thread. On the back cover, a leather lace has been attached with copper thread. To close the book, wrap the lace around the coin.

STEP THREE **PUNCH THE HOLES AND BIND THE BOOK** When the covers are completed, punch or drill holes for the rings into the two covers and pages of the book at equal distances from the edges of the book. Then add the rings, tie the leather lace, and you're done!

So you're not an artist. You don't draw, paint, sketch, or even doodle well enough for a Post-it note. Have no fear. Your journals are an expression of your personal vision, private places to create as you see fit. Sometimes, it's hard not to feel intimidated when you see other artists' journals. Remember that your personal books are not finished artwork. They're not about the results as much as they are about process. Your journals are along for the journey, whether you're the next Da Vinci or, like the rest of us, you're not. Many projects discussed in this book that create beautiful results require little or no art background.

TOP: Katy Gilmore created this book at a gathering of people who keep illustrated field journals of daily writings. ABOVE: The cover of Elizabeth Steiner's sketchbook was inspired by the colors and shapes of Central Australia. ABOVE RIGHT: "Things to Do Until I See You Again" by Roz Stendahl discusses grief and the loss of mentors, and includes jottings attempting to answer the journal's title. FAR RIGHT: Roz Stendahl's sketchbooks primarily record nature-related items, but they have grown to include anything from a precise moment in time.

notes:

Take your sketchbook everywhere, so it will be at hand when inspiration hits.

Many reprinted artists' sketchbooks are available at your local bookstore or library. Take a look at what other artists have done with their sketchbooks for inspiration with yours.

When buying or creating a sketchbook, look for thicker paper, which can better tolerate artists' materials such as watercolor, inks, and oil or acrylic paints.

LEFT: Katy Gilmore's "Commonplace Journal #9."
LEFT BELOW: Ideas and inspirations for future art projects fill Ilira Steinman's "Italy Sketchbook," created on a trip to Venice. BELOW: Marilyn R. Rosenberg's "Spirula" contains visual and verbal stylized records of Voyager, Valentine's Day roses, phases of the moon, and the rooms in the artist's home and studio. BOTTOM: Teesha Moore

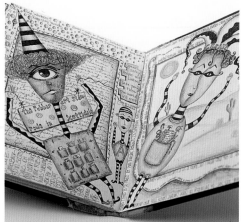

Triptychs and Books with Non-Linear Pages

MATERIALS

heavy stock paper for the cover

assorted drawing and printmaking papers

photographs

postcards

needle

bookbinding thread

binder's tape

glue

tape or other artists' materials to embellish the pages

Triptych is an ancient Greek word for early writing tablets that contained three hinged panels. In our examples, triptychs—also referred to as non-linear pages—are pages that fold outward from a journal in three parts. This technique is particularly useful for journals that aren't meant to be read from front to back. Artist Polly Smith has devised a creative binding to hold vacation mementos in her journal, "New Orleans Vacation Book." Her book has a front and back cover, but when it is opened, it reveals an unusual collection of different-size pages or leaves that can be read from left to right as well as right to left. The narrative can be read differently each time the book is opened, depending on how the reader turns the pages.

SINCE I DIDN'T HAVE TIME TO CONSTRUCT A BOOK BEFORE I LEFT ON VACATION, I BROUGHT LOOSE PAPER, PENCILS, AND WATERCOLORS WITH ME. I USED THESE MATERIALS TO CREATE THE PAGES, WHICH I LATER INDIVIDUALLY BOUND TO FLIP OPEN AND LIE FLAT.

Artist: Polly Smith

Step by Step:

ONE

TWO

STEP ONE GATHER THE PAGES Collect different-size sheets of heavy and durable artists' and printmaking papers. You may also create pages from photographs, post-cards, or other paper ephemera. The types of pages aren't as important as the collection as a whole. As the final book will contain pages of different sizes, the largest page in the group will dictate the final size of the book.

STEP TWO SEW THE PAGES Create one sewn edge on each sheet of paper in your non-linear book by sewing a blanket stitch on the binding side of your pages. The blanket stitching on each page must be of uniform distance apart, and the stitching must be wide enough for the binder's tape to slip underneath the thread.

notes:

Use different paper items for your pages such as ticket stubs, envelopes, packaging such as candy wrappers or wine labels, photographs, postcards, receipts, and paperback book covers.

The book in the step-by-step example has two sections. Try this technique with three, four, or more sections.

Add triptychs to your store-bought journals by tipping in folded pages with glue or sewing them into place with a needle and thread.

THREE   FOUR

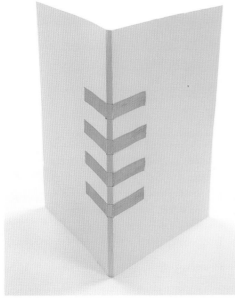

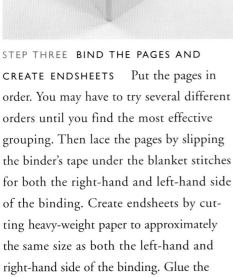

What are your dreams? Not the ones you have when you're asleep, but your desires for yourself, your family, and your future? Write down who it is you want to be, who you wish you were, your successes, and your failures. Write about your joys and personal achievements. Your journal is a quiet place where you can say what doesn't get said in everyday life. Be as honest as you can. If it's hard to open up in your daily journal, create a private one. You are who you are, and an honest journal will be more important to you in years to come than a censored one.

STEP THREE **BIND THE PAGES AND CREATE ENDSHEETS**   Put the pages in order. You may have to try several different orders until you find the most effective grouping. Then lace the pages by slipping the binder's tape under the blanket stitches for both the right-hand and left-hand side of the binding. Create endsheets by cutting heavy-weight paper to approximately the same size as both the left-hand and right-hand side of the binding. Glue the stray ends of the binder's tape onto the backside of the endsheets.

STEP FOUR **CREATE THE COVER AND ASSEMBLE THE BOOK**   The cover of your book will not only hold all the pages, but will also hide the endsheets holding the pages together. The final cover should be at least half an inch larger than the pages, so as to comfortably accommodate the endsheets. Start with a sheet of heavy stock that is as tall as the final book, but three times as wide. First, fold the cover in half. Then fold the right and left sides of the cover inward to create the pockets to slip the endsheets into. Polly Smith has sewn the folds together at the top and bottom of her book so the endsheets won't slip out when the book is read, but glue will also work. When the pockets for the endsheets are created, slip the left and right endsheets into these pockets, and you've created your non-linear book. Embellish the book cover as appropriate.

LEFT: The structure of Elizabeth Clark's accordion-fold book is analogous to the way memories tend to naturally evolve. BELOW: Juliana Cole's "Guidebook for the Distant Traveler." FACING PAGE: "Mapping Mission Creek" commemorates a place behind Roberta Lavadour's home, and includes a map that visually speaks of experience and memory.

Nature Journals

MATERIALS

fresh leaves or flowers

spray glass cleaner

inks or watercolors

paper towels

Garden journals are books that record the progress in and experiences from planting and tending gardens. One element commonly found in garden journals is leaf and flower impressions. Adding the inked impressions of favorite plants onto journal pages is a fun way to illustrate gardening successes and memories. Betty Auchard has kept leaf-impression journals for over ten years. Her journals contain plant impressions from her home in California as well as from travels throughout the United States and Canada. The technique is very simple and straightforward, and can be mastered in an afternoon. This process can also be used in daily journals to visually record places, events, or outdoor experiences.

MY SKETCHBOOKS VISUALLY RECORD MY TRAVELS THROUGHOUT NORTH AMERICA——NOT WITH PHOTOGRAPHS, BUT INSTEAD WITH COLLECTIONS OF PLANT AND LEAF IMPRESSIONS FROM THE PLACES I HAVE VISITED.

Artist: Betty Auchard

Step by Step:

LEAF IMPRESSIONS

ONE

TWO

THREE

STEP ONE PREPARE THE LEAF Begin with a fresh, dry leaf or flower. Spray the vein side of the leaf with glass cleaner to remove the natural oils that many plants contain, which may make the leaf resistant to inks or watercolors. Blot the leaf dry before continuing.

STEP TWO PAINT THE LEAF Apply ink to the vein side of the leaf. Place the leaf on your journal page, paint-side down, and carefully and gently cover with a paper towel, which will serve as a presser sheet as well as a blotter to soak up extra ink.

STEP THREE PRINT THE LEAF Press, don't rub, every part of the leaf surface. Carefully remove the paper towel and leaf to reveal the transferred image.

notes:

If you apply too much water or paint to the leaf, the final impression may smear.

Be sure to cover the entire leaf with pigment, even painting beyond the edges of the leaf. If any part of the leaf is not painted, it won't be printed.

While pressing the print by hand, hold the leaf in place with a finger at all times to keep the print from smearing.

Many books on journal-keeping that describe how and what to write can be found in your local bookstores. If you're creating a journal specifically to document your personal history, you may find these types of books inspirational. Many contain prompts to get the creative juices flowing. Try creating your own personal prompts such as the ones listed below. Keep your list somewhere in your journal to get you motivated when you find yourself staring at the blank page.

Once again, I don't know what to write. The last time this happened I ...

This is who I am today ...

This is what I did today ...

This is what I like best / least about this (journal, pen, day, place, house, life, body) ...

I keep journals because ...

I wish I was ... / I'm glad I'm not ...

If I could write in my journal to anyone it would be ...

The next artistic technique I'm going to attempt in my journal is ...

The best thing about my journal is ...

ABOVE LEFT: Betty Auchard's sketchbooks visually record her travels throughout North America without photographs, but instead with collections of plant and leaf impressions from the places she has visited. ABOVE RIGHT: Lori Kay Ludwig created this book to record the change of seasons, experienced during daily walks, following a recent relocation. TOP: Using a very simple technique, Betty Auchard's leaf transfer journals contain richly varied looks at the fauna gathered from her travels throughout North America.

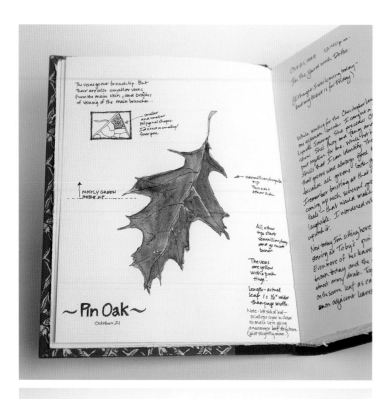

TOP LEFT: Roz Stendahl keeps sketchbooks and journals to note nature-related items, but they have grown to include anything and everything from a single precise moment. LEFT AND FACING PAGE: Peter Madden made this book over a month one spring while he was cleaning out his garden. He found thumbnail-size remnants of leaves from the previous summer and incorporated them into this piece. BELOW: After a move, Lori Kay Ludwig created this book, which she calls "Transplant," to record the change of the seasons as she experienced them during her daily walks.

Journal Techniques

Advanced journal techniques such as those found in the following chapters can help make your journal something special. Projects such as image transfers and one-of-a-kind carved stamps will help you design visually stunning pages.

The books you create should reflect your personal vision and esthetic sense, whether that be funky or arty, crafty or flowery. Like different painters using the same paints, these techniques can be utilized to create many different looks and designs, and they can be used by those of us just learning to be artistic and seasoned journalers alike. And if something doesn't work out right the first time, you can always turn the page and start again.

Wax Resist

MATERIALS

wax-based crayon or other wax source such as a candle

paint brush

water-based inks or watercolors

Wax resist is a simple and attractive technique for adding visual flair to journal pages. The materials are probably in your home or studio already, and the effect can be utilized in journals with many different themes. In the examples on these pages, artist Ilira Steinman uses wax resist as headings and sometimes complete pages for her yoga journal. The imprecise and ethereal effects resulting from the combination of wax and inks complements nicely the imagery and text of her writings.

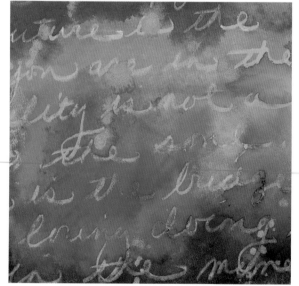

I USE MY JOURNAL AS A WAY TO RECORD MEMORABLE EXPERIENCES FROM MY WEEKLY YOGA CLASSES AS WELL AS SPECIAL SEMINARS WITH VISITING TEACHERS. SOMETIMES, I RECORD MY THOUGHTS IN A SMALL NOTEBOOK AND THEN TRANSLATE THE WRITINGS INTO VISUAL IMAGERY IN MY JOURNAL.

Artist: Ilira Steinman

Ilira Steinman created this book as a way to transcribe the inspiration she gains during her Yoga practice.

Step by Step:

WAX RESIST

ONE

TWO

THREE

STEP ONE CREATE WITH WAX In this
example, a wax crayon was used to create
the text. Note that contrasting colors
between the text and background work best.

STEP TWO START THE WASH Before
you begin to add colored ink over and
around the wax base, wet the area to allow
the ink to saturate the page completely.

**STEP THREE ADD AN INK WASH OVER
THE WAX BASE** Next, add a contrasting
ink color over the wax base. Remove any
pools of ink on top of the wax with a cotton swab or tissue paper, and allow the
page to dry.

Some people find that their best journal writing happens when they let their minds wander and forget about punctuation, grammar and spelling. When they do not see a beginning and end to an entry before they start to write, they find they are more intuitive and honest. It is one of the reasons why many journalers feel travel journals contain some of the most creative writings — our minds are full of new experiences, so we're not under pressure to decide what to write about. And at the same time, we feel compelled to write as much as possible while we're away on a travel adventure.

Paradoxically, some writers are also at their most creative when they are under pressure, perhaps because they have a specific purpose for creating in their journals. For instance, they might want to create something unique because they'll soon be seeing a friend whose journals they envy, or they might be trying to create a few outstanding first pages in their journals.

Fill your journal with a rich array of pictures as well as words. Use the wax resist technique to add colorful headings and even full-page art to journal pages. The artist Wendy Hale Davis created vivid illustrations and decorative type in wax resist to blend with her journal writing.

notes:

Different types of wax will work nicely for this technique, including beeswax, bookbinder's wax (used to coat thread), and especially crayons.

Use contrasting colors to make a more pronounced resist effect.

The effect can also be used to create backgrounds, borders, and complete pages.

Blender Pen

MATERIALS

**a blender pen
containing xylene**

binder clips

**copy machine (black
and white or color)**

bone folder

An extremely easy, flexible, and creative visual journal-keeping technique is the use of a blender pen to transfer simple images and printed text from black and white or color copies onto journal pages. Simply write out your text on your computer using an interesting font, photocopy it in reverse by using the mirror-image option, and then use a blender pen to transfer the printed text onto your journal page. You can then add color or other-wise enhance the image to create the look you desire.

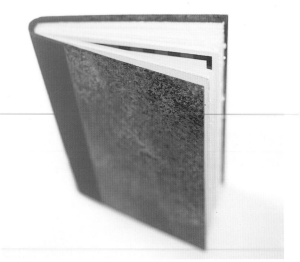

I CREATED THIS DAILY JOURNAL TO BE A VESSEL FOR EVERYDAY IDEAS, FROM THE MUNDANE TO THE NOTEWORTHY.

Artist: Jason Thompson

Step by Step:

USING A BLENDER PEN TO TRANSFER TEXT

ONE

TWO

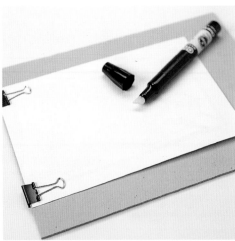

THREE

STEP ONE PRINT OR COPY IN REVERSE
Either print a master sheet in reverse and photocopy it, or use the mirror-image option on a copy machine to create a backwards image. (**Note:** Only the output from a copy machine will work because this process requires toner.)

STEP TWO USE THE BLENDER PEN
Use binder clips to attach the photocopy to your journal. Any movement of the photocopy will result in a blurred transfer. Liberally wipe the blender pen across the back of the photocopy, and press firmly against the journal page with a bone folder or other burnishing tool—you can sometimes use the back end of the blender pen if you don't have a bone folder available. Work in small areas no larger than the size of a silver dollar at a time. Allow the chemicals in the blender pen to fully saturate the photocopy.

STEP THREE REMOVE THE MASTER IMAGE AND ALLOW TO DRY Carefully peel back the photocopy to reveal the transfer. You may need to repeat the process on areas that haven't been transferred completely. (**Note:** This process will not completely remove all of the toner from your photocopy.)

Try writing from a third-person point of view. Replace "I" with "he" or "she." Write about an experience as if you were someone else, someone watching from the outside. The distance may make discussing something difficult a little easier. Try writing in your journal as if you're writing a letter. Write this letter to a friend, to the future, maybe even to the future you! Write both points of view of a topic. For instance, if you find yourself expressing negative feelings or thoughts, pretend these thoughts are part of a conversation and take another person's side, someone with a different point of view.

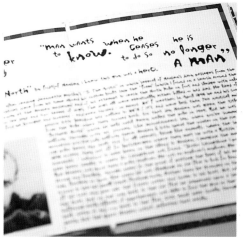

notes:

Always use a blender pen in a well-ventilated area, either inside with a fan on and the windows open, or outdoors. Read and follow all manufacturers' warnings before using any solvent.

Use your computer to lay out text onto a page the same size as your journal and transfer the entire printed page into your book.

If you only have one copy of your favorite photo or newspaper article, make a color photocopy of it and use the blender pen to transfer it into your journal.

Image Transfers

xylene solvent

bone folder

can with a lid

rags

respirator, face mask, or fan

binder clips

Note: The chemicals used in these steps can be toxic. Read all manufacturer's safety precautions before attempting these techniques.

Though the process is essentially the same as using a blender pen, using solvents to transfer images from photocopies is more involved, allows better control over the transfer, and results in a more distinct image that is less wispy. Artist Lori Kay Ludwig uses solvents to render photographs more intimate. This technique allows the repeated use of images without the need for a darkroom and permits her to be more involved with the image than a traditional photograph might.

I CREATED THIS BOOK TO RECORD MY TRANSITION TO MOTHERHOOD. IT CONTAINS IMPORTANT VISUAL RECORDS OF MY PERSONAL AND EMOTIONAL DEVELOPMENT.

Artist: Lori Kay Ludwig

6 MONTHS

Changing faster now...
skin is luminous gray...
even my face has gained
weight...
Seems as though my belly
is bigger every morning...
wonder what's there waiting...

RETAIN THIS CHECK
SEVEN
MONTHS

Baby do to my life?
...m disappear? Will
...t about ...

Step by Step:

USING SOLVENTS TO TRANSFER IMAGES

ONE

TWO

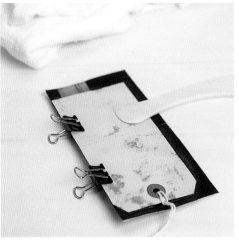

THREE

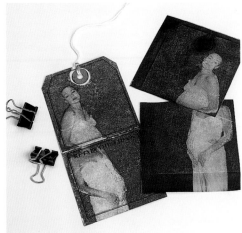

STEP ONE **PREPARE YOUR SUPPLIES** Pour about two inches of xylene into a can with a lid. Make sure your rags and burnishing tool are handy. Wear rubber gloves and a respirator, and use a fan in a well-ventilated area, or work outside. Place your photo-copied image face-down onto the page and clip into place with binder clips.

STEP ONE **APPLY THE SOLVENT** Dip the rag into the can. The rag should be thoroughly wet but not dripping. Rub the solvent onto the backside of your photo-copy, covering a small section of the image at a time. Burnish each section as you go with your burnishing tool. Take a peek every so often to see which areas need to be burnished again. Don't be surprised if you need to apply solvent to or burnish an area a few times before you achieve the desired effect.

STEP THREE **REMOVE THE PHOTO-COPY** Remove the binder clips and peel away the photocopy. In some places, the toner may have adhered the paper, leaving tiny, thin, threadlike bits on the image when the pho-tocopy is peeled back. This is considered an advantage, as it lends a hand-drawn appear-ance to your final image. You can now enhance the image with colored pencils, charcoal, pastel, watercolor—whatever works best with your own journal.

Some journals are kept in chronological order, starting on the first page and ending on the last page, while some have entries arbitrarily entered throughout the book. If you're intimidated by the first blank page in a book, try creating your first entry somewhere in the middle of the book, or start your journal the same way every time. For example, you might always begin your journal with a page describing who you are, where you are, and how you obtained or made the book: what fabric you used, how long it took to bind, where you made it. You might also write about the last journal you kept, how much time it spanned, and what you liked about it. After you've made the first entry, you'll feel less apprehensive about the prospect of all those blank pages.

The images in this book were found vacation photos discovered in antique shops. All the images show cobblestones in them. Artist: Roberta Lavadour

notes:

Always use solvents such as xylene in a well-ventilated area, either inside with a fan on and the windows open, or outdoors.

Other solvents besides xylene will work to transfer images, and can also produce results of a different opacity and hue. Try this technique using acetone, lighter fluid, hairspray, peppermint oil, or denatured alcohol.

Try adding transfer images from a special trip into a travel journal, baby pictures into a new baby journal, or pictures of friends and family into a daily journal to document the people in your life.

Sewing and Non-Adhesive Inclusions

MATERIALS

needle, thread or other sewing material

scissors

When we want to attach items onto journal pages, the first thing that comes to mind is glue. Adhesives are transparent; they're the medium, not part of the composition. Sewing, however, is part of the composition. To include more texture to journal pages, artist Peter Madden decoratively sews meaningful objects into his journals and artist books. In his journal, "Relic," Peter has collected items from his past, his family, and places he's visited, and catalogued them into book form. The technique is very straightforward, and sewing experience is not necessary. Furthermore, as sewing showcases the thread, you can use the thread as a decorative element.

THIS SCRAPBOOK, CALLED "RELIQUIAE II," IS A MEANS OF PRESERVING AND DESCRIBING A COLLECTION OF PERSONAL ESOTERICA.

Artist: Peter Madden

ABOVE: Peter Madden's "Reliquiae II"

rel·ic (rel´ik) n. [ME. relike < OFr. relique < L. reliquiae, pl., remains] 1. a) an object, custom, etc. that has survived, wholly or partially from the past b) something that has historical interest because of its age and associations with the past, or that serves as a keepsake, or souvenir 2. [pl.] remaining fragments; surviving parts; ruins.

Step by Step:

ONE

TWO

THREE

STEP ONE **SEW AROUND ORGANIC MATERIALS**   In this example, Peter has sewn rose stems into his book. Note how the thread creates a unique pattern along the stems.

STEP TWO **SEW IN A POCKET**   The thread in this example not only creates a pattern along the edge of the lace that forms a pocket, but also follows the theme of the needle and thread underneath the lace.

STEP THREE **SEW IN EPHEMERA**   The simple technique of sewing in paper ephemera adds dimension to these otherwise visually simple elements. Note also that in the three examples here, the pages of Peter's books are themselves sewn together. This is not only a design element but also allows the ends of the threads to be hidden between the pages.

notes:

Try sewing with thread, twine, wire, raffia, plastic ties, yarn, embroidery floss, string, or ribbon.

If you're concerned about the stray ends of the thread, let both ends terminate underneath the page you're working on, and secure and hide the trailing ends on the backside with tape or a collage or some other visual element.

To create neatly executed sewn patterns, mark your journal page with a template before actually piercing the page with the needle.

Where do you write? Do you write all the time? Only at set times and only in certain places? If it helps to inspire you, try setting aside either a place or a time to write and create on a regular basis. Maybe you write before you go to bed, or you have a small studio with your art supplies. Perhaps you find yourself inspired to create at random moments during the day. If so, keep your journal with you at all times. Write during your morning coffee, on the train to work, during lunch, at school, after work, or at home alone. Creating a special place where you feel comfortable can be inspiration enough to get your journal and journaling supplies together.

ABOVE: This is the original book of artists Judy and Mallory Serebrin's collaborative series. RIGHT: This collaborative book is the second in a series that began as a birthday present from Mallory Serebrin to her sister Judy. Both women are artists and send the book back and forth to help them stay connected.

TOP AND LEFT: Judy Serebrin's daily journal traveled with her from Seattle to Israel. BELOW: Peter Madden's journals embody themes of memory and loss. BELOW LEFT: Peter Madden's hand-bound book with hammered copper on wood covers has mixed-media pages with computer-generated text. FACING PAGE TOP: "Memories Revisited" by Maria Pisano commemorates the daily life of the artist's parents, capturing moments that were not necessarily highlights, but celebrated who they were. FACING PAGE BELOW: This book, called "Big Book III," is very different from the others Juliana Coles has created. She works in this book with her students during classes.

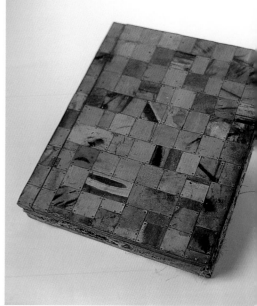

Paper Cutting

MATERIALS

matte knife

ruler

cutting mat

pencil

eraser

The idea of making cuts in journal pages to allow photographs to be added to them came simply from wanting to place a photograph onto a page of a journal and not having either a glue stick, photocorners, or tape available. It quickly became apparent, however, that this creative technique can be used to add visual interest to journal pages even if the option of using glue or photocorners is available. The concept is straightforward, and yet there are limitless creative combinations. The technique is particularly great to use in a travel journal. On these pages, you'll find a few examples of cut pages with photographs as well as other objects inserted into journals using the same technique.

WHILE SEARCHING FOR A LOFT IN PROVIDENCE, RHODE ISLAND, I CREATED THIS BOOK AS A PLACE TO STORE INFORMATION SUCH AS ADDRESSES, REALTORS' NUMBERS, AND PICTURES OF BUILDINGS.

Artist: Jason Thompson

Imminent Demolition

WE FOUND THIS FEATHER IN THE STUDIO.

ARE BIRDS SQUATTING HERE AT NIGHT?

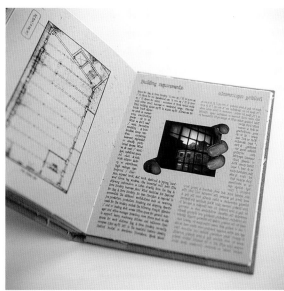

one allen avenue
march to june
19:9:8

before / during / after

THE DAY WE SAID, "WE'LL TAKE IT!"

MARCH 25th, 1998

"WE'LL TAKE IT!"

04/06/98

04/30/98

Step by Step:

PAPER CUTTING

ONE   TWO   THREE

STEP ONE   **CREATE THE BACKGROUND**

In this example, a black and white image of a hand holding a picture will form the frame around the photograph that is to be inserted into the journal. Once cut, the fingers will serve as photocorners, holding the photograph in place.

STEP TWO   **CUT THE BACKGROUND**

Outline the photograph with a pencil to form the edges that will be cut out of the page. Next, cut around all of the portions of the black and white image that will show over the photograph.

STEP THREE   **PLACE THE PHOTOGRAPH**

Erase any pencil marks that may show around the finished layout. Slip the photograph into the slots formed by the cuts.

After looking through so many journals created by different artists and journalers, we've discovered some common elements among them that you may find in your own journals.

INSPIRATION Many journalers sew or glue items of inspiration into their journals such as images from other journaler's books, postcards from gallery and art exhibits, pictures from magazines, photographs, or inspirational quotes and writings.

PICTURES OF PETS Somehow cat and dog pictures always make it into our journals.

COFFEE RINGS It's almost a requirement to have a coffee-cup ring in your journal.

HAPPY AND SAD Journalers often find their deepest inspiration when writing about tragedies and triumphs.

FIRST PERSON Who do you write to? Many journalers like to write to themselves.

THIS BOOK BELONGS TO: Don't forget this one. I once left my journal in a rental truck, and the next person who rented the truck called me to say they had found it!

ABOVE AND RIGHT: Roberta Lavadour created this book to commemorate a place along a creek behind her home. The book contains a map, which visually speaks of experience and memory instead of geography.

notes:

To permanently use cutout pages to showcase photographs in your journal, place a bit of glue or double-sided tape to the back of larger photographs.

Cut corners don't have to be used to hold photographs. Try using them to add flowers, feathers, currency, stamps, or other ephemera to your journal.

Remember that the other side of your page will show portions of your photograph poking through. To hide these corners, paste a collage or something special on the page.

More Than Handwriting

MATERIALS

newspaper or magazines

scissors

rubber stamps

pens

pencils

paints

brushes

Artist Maura Cluthe creates beautiful, simple, everyday journals utilizing many visual elements, including text-based entries that contain more than handwriting. She adds words to her journals using techniques that include copying and pasting typed entries and using rubber-stamp alphabets. These techniques give more weight to the words she uses by making them more visual. Pictures alone may also convey dialogue, just as words can be used to create visual elements, as seen in the examples here.

I CARRY SKETCHBOOKS WITH ME TO RECORD WHAT I

SEE AS A STARTING POINT FOR LARGER WORKS.

Artist: Maura Cluthe

Artist: Maura Cluthe

Step by Step:

MORE THAN HANDWRITING

ONE

TWO

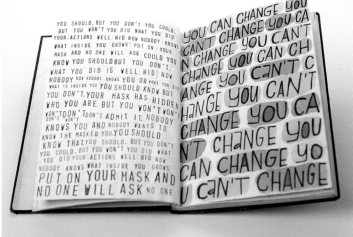

This book contains ideas and inspiration for larger works of art. It's one of the sketchbooks Maura Cluthe says she carries with her everywhere.

THREE

STEP ONE **USE RUBBER STAMPS**
Though it takes more time, using a rubber-stamp alphabet is a distinct way to add words to your journal pages. Try using different sets of stamps or different-colored stamp pads.

STEP TWO **CUT AND PASTE** Try cutting and pasting text printed from a computer. Use unusual fonts, move the text around the page, and explore different sizes and colors for the words.

STEP THREE **SAY IT LOUD!** Different-size text entries can convey different volumes of speech, just as in real life. The bigger, the louder; the smaller, the quieter. Use text that complements what you're trying to say.

These journals are from Teesha Moore's Everyday Journal series. TOP AND RIGHT: "Everyday Journal #3." ABOVE: "Everyday Journal #1."

A definite vision will help inspire you when you don't feel like creating. Think of how you would answer if a friend asked you why you keep a journal. Do you keep it for the memories? For the art? Because it's inspirational or therapeutic? Maybe you find yourself drawn to journals and don't know why. Perhaps you saw someone else's books and were inspired to keep your own. Think about what your reasons are and write them down in every journal you create. Revisit your answers when you find yourself with creator's block.

notes:

If you're bored with writing entries in your journals from left to right, try writing sideways, upside-down, along the gutter, or across the entire two-page spread.

Mix things up by using different techniques to add words to a page, allowing the words themselves to become visual elements.

Try using dymo tape; cutouts from newspapers and magazines; and even copies of Web sites, computer images, or the handwriting of your friends and family.

Plaster Paper

MATERIALS

dry stretched paper

spackle

spackle knife

sandpaper

dust mask

texturing tools

acrylic paint

wax

spray-mount adhesive

Surface treatments give journal pages an extra layered element and visual interest. One of the most unusual surface treatments is Melissa Slattery's plaster paper technique. This unique process creates a distressed and "shabby chic" look. This technique lends itself well to pages that contain minimal text entries or to travel journals with specific color schemes. For instance, a visit to Sienna, Italy, may inspire you to create journal pages with sienna hues to them. Rich colors also look fabulous. Try this technique out for yourself and see what types of creative entries it inspires.

THIS BOOK CONTAINS PAGES CREATED WITH MY PLASTER PAPER TECHNIQUE. IT IS A TRAVEL JOURNAL OF SORTS, WITH ARTWORK CREATED WITH PASTEL, GRAPHITE, AND COLLAGE, AMONG OTHER TECHNIQUES.

Artist: Melissa Slattery

BOStON, 1992, Nov 15
Temperatures soared into
the 70°'s. We rented
a car and Drove to Waltham,
...Thickly settled.

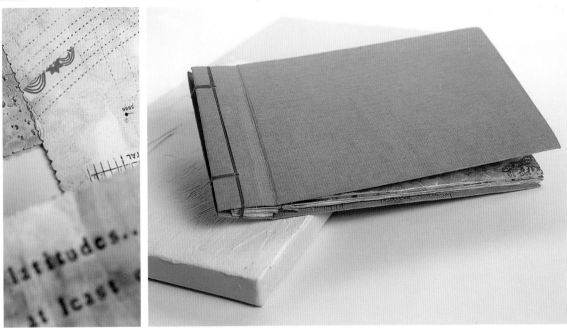

Artist: Mellissa Slattery

Step by Step:

ONE	TWO	THREE

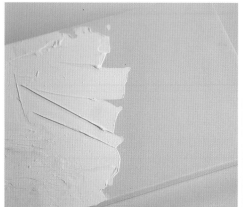

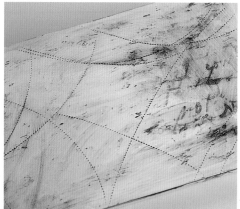

STEP ONE **APPLY THE SPACKLE** Either stretch the paper you wish to work on or, if you are working directly in a journal, use a spray-mount adhesive to temporarily attach a backer such as Davey board, a bookbinder's board used to create hardcovers, to the under-side of your page to prevent warping. Before working directly in your journal, however, you might wish to practice this technique on a piece of scrap paper first. Apply a thin layer of spackle with a putty knife, making sure not to apply too much.

STEP TWO **SAND AND CREATE TEXTURE** Lightly sand the surface with a fine-grade sandpaper to smooth away any deep grooves. To add texture to your page, create patterns on or distress the spackle as it is drying. Allow the spackle to dry before continuing. Once the plaster is sanded and dry, you can begin to add color to the surface with acrylic paint, watercolors, inks, shoe polish, or graphite.

STEP THREE **FINALIZE THE DESIGN** Once color has been added, you can rubber-stamp, collage, paint, or even incise the surface with linoleum or wood-block cutting tools to create the look you desire.

notes:

Because this process creates thick pages, use this technique in an expandable journal with heavy pages, or bind your own book with the pages after they've been created.

Try adding a liberal amount of beeswax to "crayonize" the surface. Remove excess beeswax with a spatula, and polish with a soft cloth.

Cover any collaged images with a matte-finish, clear-coat spray enamel and allow to dry.

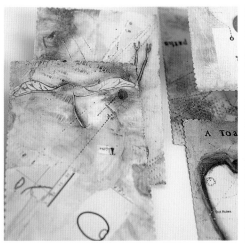

You don't have to keep a journal faithfully. Some people keep journals on and off during their lives, sometmes going years without writing. There are times in life when you might not need to keep a journal, so do your best not to feel guilty when you're not writing or creating in one. Time will pass, and then one day you will find an old journal (or maybe it will find you), and the process begins again. There will always be a blank book waiting for us at any given time in our lives. Journal keeping shouldn't be a chore, it should be a release. Think of your journals as friends who are always there for you, not simply as appointments that must be kept.

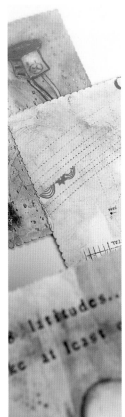

Created with Mellissa Slattery's plaster paper technique, these artistic 'cards' are enclosed in a wax paper folder and tied with measuring tape ribbon.

Emulsion Lifts

MATERIALS

camera that uses pack film

pack film

candy thermometer

tea kettle

glass or Pyrex trays to hold water

contact or shelf paper

scissors

wax paper

clear-coat spray enamel

brayer or bone folder

An exciting and advanced technique for adding photographic imagery to your journals is a process called an emulsion lift. This involved process requires lifting or removing the very delicate emulsion from photograph paper and then adhering it to your journal pages. One of the nice results of this technique is that the transferred emulsion is so thin that you can barely feel that it's there, but the image remains vivid and crisp. Lori Kay Ludwig uses emulsion lifts extensively in her journals. In the example here, she has utilized an altered book to create a journal documenting the changing of the seasons which contains emulsion lifts almost exclusively, even on the cover.

I CREATED THIS ONE-OF-A-KIND ARTISTS' BOOK TO RECORD THE MONTH OF OCTOBER 1999.

Artist: Lori Kay Ludwig

BELOW: This is a solvent transfer. BOTTOM: This emulsion-lift monthly journal is a hand-bound, recycled arithmetic book from 1852.

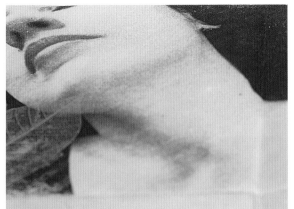

Step by Step:

ONE

TWO

STEP ONE **HEAT THE WATER** Note that this process only works with cameras that use pack film, a special film by Polaroid that is the only type of film that works with this technique. Ask your local camera shop for more information regarding cameras that use this type of film. Pour a tea kettle's worth of water that is exactly 160 degrees Fahrenheit (71 degrees Celsius) into the tray. Carefully monitor the water's temperature with the thermometer. Adhere contact or shelf paper to the back of the photograph to prevent the backing of the print from dissolving in the water.

STEP TWO **IMMERSE THE PHOTO-GRAPH IN WATER** Submerge your photograph in the water for approximately four minutes. During this time, you should start to see bubbles form underneath the image, and the edges will start to loosen. Gently rock the tray if necessary to hasten the process.

Creating lists is a way to keep a personal inventory of who and where we are at any given moment. Try creating a list of who you are at different times in your life. For example, I am a husband, artist, diarist, computer user, mediator, son, writer, webmaster, cat lover, boss, employer, bookbinder, and friend. See how these lists change as you enter different phases in your life. Look back on them and see if the person you were years ago is the same as the person you are now.

THREE

FOUR

STEP THREE REMOVE THE EMULSION
When the emulsion starts to peel away from the photograph, carefully float the emulsion on top of a clean sheet of wax paper and flatten any wrinkles or creases. Next, carefully remove the wax paper and the emulsion from the water.

STEP FOUR PLACE THE EMULSION INTO YOUR JOURNAL Carefully lift the thin layer of emulsion off the wax paper and place it onto your journal page. It may crease, crinkle, or even tear. Be prepared to accept these effects as part of your composition. Press the image lightly with a brayer to remove any water or air bubbles from beneath its surface and seal with a spray enamel.

notes:

This process creates very vivid and clear images in such an unusual way that you should consider using the images for special pages or even the cover of your journal.

Try playing around with the way the emulsion crinkles and folds as it is transferred.

The ethereal effect of emulsion-lift transfers looks great in dream journals!

Carved Stamps

MATERIALS

**large eraser or
wine cork**

**carving tools such
as linoleum or
wood-carving knives**

ink

Although a few early entrepreneurs have claimed
the title, no one knows who created the first rubber stamp. Suffice it to say, today's rubber stamps
have come a long way from those created to ease
the printing bills of manufacturers in the 1800s.
Artist Teesha Moore not only uses many rubber
stamps in her journals but even sells her own line
of stamps to other journalers and artists. The
stamps she creates are unique and showcase her
own particular vision. We will show you how to
create your very own one-of-a-kind, custom-made
eraser and cork stamps.

THESE ARE MY CREATIVE PLAYGROUND JOURNALS. AS FAR

AS A THEME GOES, THE QUOTE, "ART AND LIFE ARE ONE,"

COMES TO MIND. I DO WHAT I FEEL LIKE ON THE PAGES

FOR THAT PARTICULAR DAY WITH NO RULES.

Artist: Teesha Moore

Teesha Moore's hand-stamped art journals include Everyday
Journals #1 and #3.

Step by Step:

ONE

TWO

STEP ONE ERASER STAMPS: DRAW YOUR OUTLINE Draw an outline of the image you wish to cut on the eraser. Try simple forms to begin with. If you're a better writer than artist, you can use a blender pen to transfer computer-generated text or images onto the surface of the stamp. Remember that the image on the stamp must be carved in reverse! Using a small, sharp blade, carefully carve away the eraser around your image. Cut outward from your image to avoid undercutting your stamp.

STEP TWO PRINT! When you've finished carving, practice stamping a few times and remove any unwanted portions of the eraser that are visible when stamped. The print from a cork stamp leaves a more distressed impression, which creates an artful effect.

notes:

Paint different-colored inks onto single stamps for a more colorful effect.

To create stamps with two or more colors, carve identical stamps with different portions removed. Print the first stamp in one color, and the second in another, carefully lining up the stamps when you print.

Create a set of alphabet or number stamps out of cork for making headings, dates, and page numbers in your journals.

ONE

TWO

STEP ONE CORK STAMPS: DRAW YOUR
OUTLINE   To create interesting, carved
wine corks, begin with a cork that has a flat
surface. If the surface of the cork isn't flat,
it won't print correctly. If necessary, you can
use a sharp blade to slice off the top or bottom of a cork prior to carving. Draw the
image you wish to carve on the cork. Cutting cork is harder than carving an eraser.
Be sure to use a sharp blade, and handle it
carefully when you are cutting.

STEP TWO PRINT!

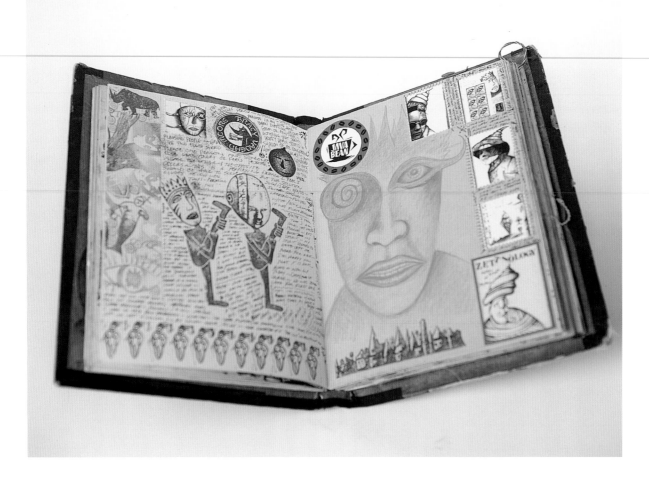

If you have concerns about creating a perfect journal, or if you find the blank page intimidating, spread your ideas out by keeping a diary, a journal, and a sketchbook simultaneously. Your diary may contain mostly written entries, and you should write in it regularly. Your journal can be a place to experiment with different artistic techniques like the ones taught in this book. And your sketchbook can be a place for you to flesh out ideas for other artistic works such as paintings or illustrations.

FACING PAGE: Teesha Moore's Everyday Journal #1
ABOVE: Peter Madden's tray of cork stamps. LEFT AND
BOTTOM: Teesha Moore's Everyday Journal #1

Journals as Art

MATERIALS

water color

inks

tape

glue

acrylic paint

gesso

crayons

colored pencils, etc.

For some journalers, when the creative process fully opens up and they begin to completely express themselves in their journals, their books become works of art. This is especially the case with the journals of Juliana Coles, which contain thoughts and dreams from her daily life. Though the visual and written elements in her books are confessional, reading them isn't voyeuristic; she simply wants to share herself with others, and her journals are the medium. In these examples, we can see how a personal journal, though essentially private, can be created with the knowledge that it will be shared with others, and should rightfully be considered a work of art.

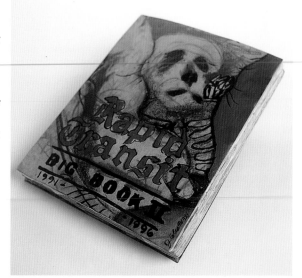

THIS BOOK IS VERY DIFFERENT FROM THE OTHERS I HAVE CREATED. I WORK IN THIS BOOK WITH MY STUDENTS DURING CLASSES. IN IT I DON'T FEEL CONSTRAINED TO BE AN ARTIST. IT'S MORE PLAYFUL, LESS HEAVY.

Artist: Juliana Coles

ABOVE AND LEFT: Juliana Coles' journal began as an artist sketchbook, which over time turned into a visual journal containing self portraits, dreams, ideas for project and poems.

Step by Step:

JOURNALS AS ART

ONE

TWO

THREE

STEP ONE **SKETCH YOURSELF IN A SELF-PORTRAIT** Self portraits are extremely personal and revealing, saying a great deal about a person and their state of mind. Self-portraits from different periods of your life can reveal different messages that you may only fully understand after the passage of time.

STEP TWO **SAY WHAT YOU FEEL** If you expect others to read your journals, you may be more inclined to say and write what you might otherwise consider obvious. Words of wisdom, which may ordinarily be scattered throughout your journal entries, can become entire pages supported by appropriate visual elements. You are special in your own way and have your own vision—share it with the world.

STEP THREE **RETELL YOUR STORIES** The stories and experiences from your own life can be written in a manner other than a first-person narrative. For instance, Juliana Coles expressed her narratives in visual form. Some of these pages contain graphic novel–type panels, and others are written in unusual scripts that convey more than just what the words say—the colors, the images, and the layout all help to further express her thoughts.

notes:

Can't draw? Try collage or using rubberstamps, or create images on a computer and use a blender pen or solvents to transfer them onto your journal pages. Use these images as a basis for creative entries.

Creating an entry without words is a great way to visualize your own thoughts. You may be surprised by the outcome.

Try working in a medium you're not familiar with. Take pictures if you're not a photographer, for example, or try your hand at watercolors if you haven't done so before.

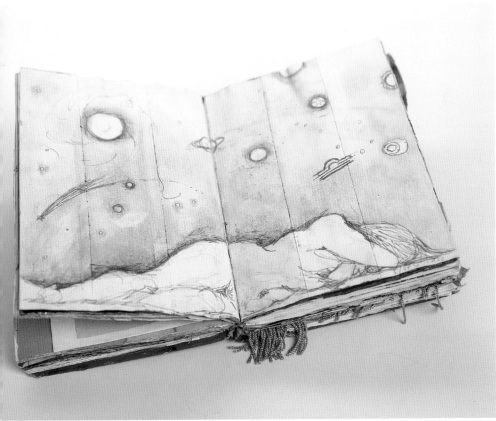

A fine pen and a blank journal make a wonderful gift for a child. Show your own journal to others, and maybe you will inspire them to start keeping a journal, too. Here are a few suggestions for giving a blank book to a friend or family member:

HAND-BOUND BLANK BOOK Make one yourself if you can.

PEN AND INK Fountain pens along with a bottle of ink make great gifts.

JOURNAL SUPPLIES Colored pencils, a glue stick, photocorners, watercolors, a paint brush, and other artists' supplies will help inspire different ways of using a journal. Look through the materials list chapter for more inspiration.

JOURNAL BOX Put all of these items into a portable box, such as an artist's wooden paint box, or even decorate a small carrying case.

ABOVE: Juliana Coles used this book as a creative journal to follow along with writer Julia Cameron's *The Artist's Way* exercises. ABOVE LEFT: Juliana created this book to contain less serious artwork. It is a playful journal with many items attached to the pages.

Thinking Outside the Book

Webster's American English dictionary defines the word book as "a set of written, printed, or blank sheets bound together into a volume." Though we generally picture "bound" as including two covers and a spine, there are many ways to bind together sheets to form a volume. In fact, as seen in the examples here, collecting or assembling our thoughts or daily writings together does not require the use of a traditional book. The examples by Roz Stendahl and Ilira Steinman demonstrate that a box can hold entries. You could also use an embellished metal can or a clay vessel. For a creative thinker, thinking outside the book can lead to wonderful, non-traditional interpretations of what a journal can be.

FACING PAGE: Roz Stendahl creates collages out of artifacts from her daily life and keep them in a box. ABOVE LEFT AND RIGHT: Artist Ilira Steinman created this boxed collection of cards for her boyfriend, now husband, to read one card a day while she was away in Italy. BELOW LEFT AND RIGHT: Jeanne Minnix's "Wishing Well: Hopes and Dreams."

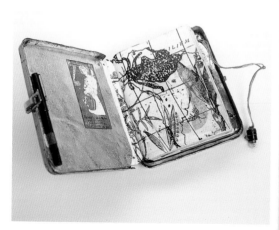

FACING PAGE, TOP AND BOTTOM LEFT: Raphael Lyon's book was created as a multipurpose journal for collecting and researching eth-nobotony in the Brazillian Rainforest. THIS PAGE AND FACING PAGE, BOTTOM RIGHT: Deborah Waimon says she is drawn to the work of, "Beauty…" and the frayed covers of this vintage book communicates a sense of purpose. Reconstructing the book into a box has given it new life.

Ornaments are everywhere! This box, with its flip-top lid and many compartments, can hold collections of all sorts—pens and pen nibs, marbles, costume jewelry, sea shells, special holiday decorations. The Ornament Box is a wonderful vehicle for papers (such as gift wrap papers) too fragile to wrap around the walls of a tray. Cloth does all of the hard work here; decorative papers are pasted on top of the cloth in the final step to give the box its visual punch. I have used an inexpensive Italian Bertini paper because I like its geometric pattern and simple one-color printing. Some of the papers are more typically Florentine, with flourishes and highlights of gold.

   The Ornament Box consists of a four-walled tray with partitions and a hinged lid. The lid is actually an upside-down three-walled tray.

the ornament box...
memories of a collector's passions

MATERIALS

Binder's board

Bookcloth

Decorative paper

PVA, mixture and paste

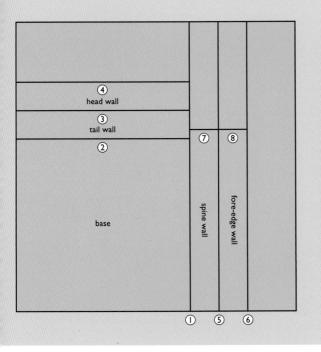

Diagram labels:
- ④ head wall
- ③ tail wall
- ②
- base
- ⑦ spine wall
- ⑧ fore-edge wall
- ① ⑤ ⑥
- grain

getting started:
cutting the boards for the tray

- Cut out the boards for the tray, following the layout.
- Base:
  Height = desired height of tray, plus two cloth thicknesses
  Width = desired width of tray, plus two cloth thicknesses
- Head and tail walls:
  Height = desired depth of tray, plus one board thickness
  Width = desired width of tray, plus two cloth thicknesses
  (same as width of base board)
- Spine and fore-edge walls:
  Height = height of base board, plus two board thicknesses
  Width = desired depth of tray, plus one board thickness
  (same as height of head and tail walls)

1a, b   **CONSTRUCT THE TRAY**
(see The Basics, page 122). Glue the walls
in the proper sequence: head, fore-edge,
tail, then spine.

1b

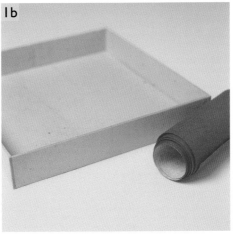

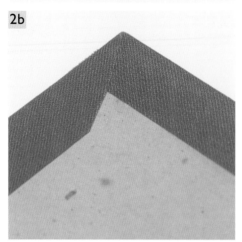

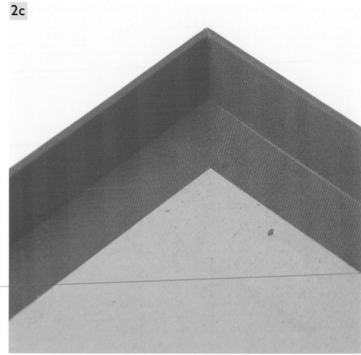

2a–c **COVER THE TRAY.** Cut a strip of bookcloth to a measurement of twice the depth of the tray plus 1 1/2" (4 cm), and long enough to wrap around all four walls plus 1/2" (1 cm).

2d   Cover the tray (see The Basics, page 123).

3a

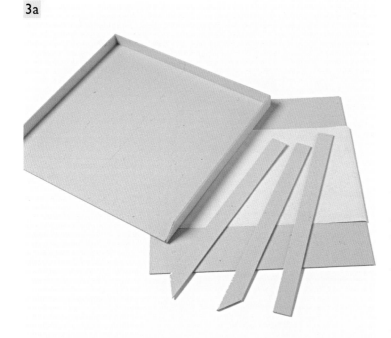

3b

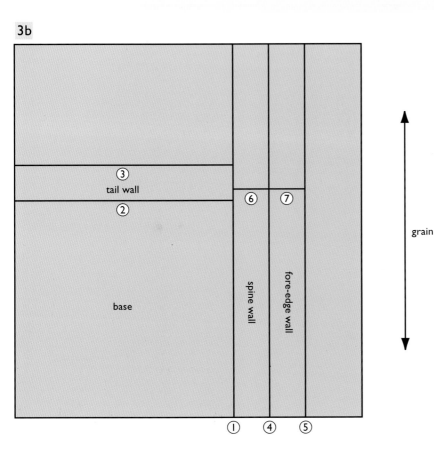

base

③
tail wall

②

⑥   ⑦

spine wall

fore-edge wall

①   ④   ⑤

grain

3a, b CUT OUT THE BOARDS for the
lid, following the lay-out below. The lid is
a three-walled tray, inverted over the lower
tray and hinged to it at the back (head)
wall. There is no head wall to the lid.
Because the lid takes its measurements
from the covered tray, start by squaring
a piece of board (see The Basics, page
122), and placing the tray on the squared
corner. Mark the board, and cut:
Base:
Height = height of tray plus two cloth
thicknesses
Width = width of tray plus two cloth
thicknesses
Tail wall:
Height = desired depth of lid plus one
board thickness
Width = width of tray plus two cloth
thicknesses (same as width of base)
Spine and fore-edge walls:
Height = height of base plus two board
thicknesses
Width = desired depth of lid plus one
board thickness (same as height of tail wall)

NEXT   CONSTRUCT THE LID. Angle
the ends of the spine and fore-edge walls.
Glue up the tray (see The Basics, page
122), starting with the tail wall and proceeding to the spine and fore-edge walls.

4a

4b

4c

4d

4a COVER THE LID.

4b Cut a strip of bookcloth to a measurement of twice the depth of the tray plus 1¹/₂" (4 cm), and long enough to wrap around all three walls plus 1¹/₂" (4 cm).

4c, d Cover the tray, following the same procedure as for covering a four-walled tray (see The Basics, page 21). Allow a ³/₄" (2 cm) turn-in at the angled edges of the spine and fore-edge walls.

4e, f Do not glue these turn-ins onto the board until the tray has been wrapped and the appropriate cuts have been made (see diagram).

4e

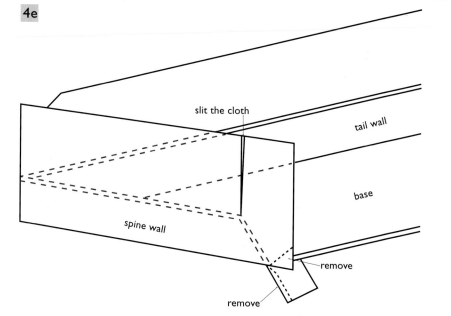

slit the cloth

tail wall

base

spine wall

remove

remove

4f

5   ATTACH THE LID TO THE TRAY.
Cut two hinge strips from the bookcloth, both to the same dimensions:
Height = 1 1/2" (4 cm)
Width = width of tray (outside)
One hinge connects the lid to the tray on the outside, at the head wall. The second hinge covers the lid-to-tray attachment on the inside.

Place the lid on the tray. Glue out one hinge. Stick it down, 3/4" (2 cm) onto the lid and centered. Press with your bone folder. Shape the cloth against the right angle formed by the lid and the head wall of the tray, and press the cloth down well, against the wall. Let the box sit closed, for 10 to 15 minutes.

Open the lid and roll the box onto its head wall. Place the second hinge (unglued) in the box, centered over the joint space between the lid and the tray. Trim slivers of cloth off each end so that the cloth fits perfectly inside the tray. Glue out this strip and stick it down. Immediately force the cloth into the joint with a bone folder. Rub vigorously until the cloth is well-adhered to all surfaces. Let the box sit open, for a few minutes, then close the box and let it sit under weights for 1/2 hour.

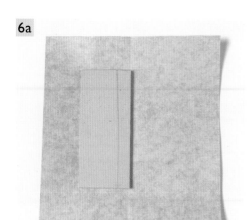

6a

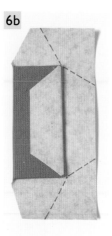

6b

6c

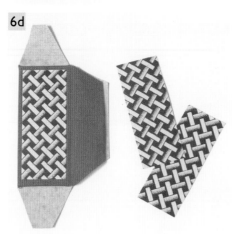

6d

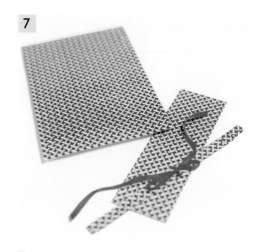

7

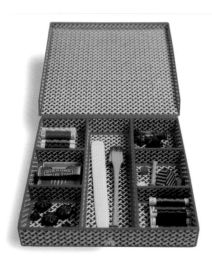

6a-d   MAKE AND ADHERE THE PAR-TITION WALLS. (See the Tip on the next page)

Mark the base of the tray for their placement.

Glue out the bottom flanges of each partition and adhere the partition to the base. When the glue has begun to set, apply glue to the side flanges and press them onto the tray walls.

Note: It is easier to line the partition walls with decorative paper before gluing them into the box. In my box, the two long partitions must be lined after all of the partitions are attached in order to hide the flanges from the short partitions. All of the short partitions, however, can be covered before attaching them—and that is what I did. Depending on the configuration of your walls, you must make your own decision.

7   LINE THE BOX. Cut strips of decorative paper to line the lid and tray walls (inside and out). Apply adhesive and stick them down. Cut pieces of decorative paper to cover the floors of all the compartments. Apply adhesive and stick them down. Cut one piece of either paper or bookcloth to line the bottom of the box (outside). Apply adhesive and stick it down. Cut two pieces of paper to cover and line the lid. Apply adhesive to these papers and stick them down. With the box open and sitting on its head wall, press the lid by filling it with newsprint and weights. Leave for several hours, until dry.

Tip: How to Make Partition Boards

 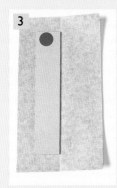  

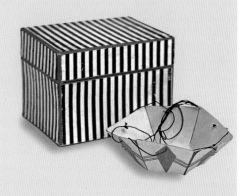

All of the four-walled projects described in this book (the Candy, Jewelry, and Letter boxes) can have partition walls built into them. Just remember that the flanges attaching the partitions to the tray should be disguised somehow. In The Ornament Box, the walls are covered with strips of decorative paper to hide the construction details. If the tray and walls are covered in a patterned paper—the busier the better—this protective coloration will help the flanges disappear into the walls. The models above illustrate the ten steps in making partitions.

1. Cut out the partitions. The boards should fit from wall to wall with a little breathing room. In depth, they should be shallower than the interior depth of the tray by one board thickness.

2. Cut out the cloth or covering paper:
Height = height of board plus 1 1/2" (4 cm)
Width = twice the width of the board plus 1 1/2" (4 cm)
Crease the cloth in half lengthwise.

3. Glue out the board and position it on the cloth against the crease mark; center it heightwise. Press.

4. Cut corners off the cloth, at the head and tail near the 3/4" (2 cm) turn-ins only. Keep cuts one-and-a-half board thicknesses away from the tips of the board.

5. Remove triangular wedges of cloth from the head and tail turn-ins, at the creased center of the bookcloth. Cut in close to the board.

6. Glue the head and tail turn-ins, bringing them onto the board and pinching in the cloth at the corners.

7. Glue out the board and roll it onto the right-hand half of the creased cloth. Press it down well.

8. Cut corners off the cloth at the head and tail.

9. Sharply fold the four cloth extensions backward, onto themselves, to form the flanges.

10. If desired, line the partitions with decorative paper. (See the Note in Step 6.)

RESOURCES

WHERE TO BUY BLANK BOOKS:

Paper Source Inc.
232 West Chicago Avenue
Chicago, IL 60610
(312) 337-0798

Rugg Road Paper Company
105 Charles Street
Boston, MA 02114
(617) 742-0002

Kate's Paperie
561 Broadway
New York, NY 10012
(212) 941-9816
www.katespaperie.com

Flax Art & Design
240 Valley Drive
Brisbane, CA 94005-1206
1-800-343-FLAX
www.flaxart.com

Papyrus
2500 N. Watney Way
Fairfield, CA 94533
1-800-333-6724
www.papyrus-stores.com

Soolip Paperie
8646 Melrose Avenue
West Hollywood, CA 90069
(310) 360-0545

Two Hands Paperie
803 Pearl Street
Boulder, CO 80302
(303) 444-0124
www.twohandspaperie.com

The Written Word
1365 Connecticut Avenue
Washington, D.C. 20036
(202) 223-1400

Borders Books
1-800-770-7811
www.borders.com

Barnes & Noble
1-800-THE-BOOK
www.barnesandnoble.com

WHERE TO BUY JOURNALING MATERIALS:

Sam Flax
12 West 20th Street
New York, NY 10011
(212) 620-3038

A I Freidman
44 W. 18th Street
New York, NY 10011
(212) 243-9000

Pearl Arts and Crafts
225 W. Chicago Avenue
Chicago, IL 60610
(312) 915-0200

Michaels Crafts
P.O. Box 619566
Dallas Fort Worth, TX 75261-9566
(972) 409-1300
www.michaels.com

WHERE TO BUY BOX-MAKING MATERIALS:

Adams Magnetic Products
2081 North 15th Avenue
Melrose Park, IL 60160
(800) 222-6686
Fax: (708) 681-1879
Magnetic strips and sheets

Aiko's Art Material Import, Inc.
3347 North Clark Street
Chicago, IL
(312) 404-5600
Fax: (312) 404-5919
Japanese paper; bookcloth; tools; books
on bookbinding; general art materials

American Graphic Arts, Inc.
150 Broadway
Elizabeth, NJ 07206
(908) 351-6906
Fax: (909) 351-7156
Reconditioned bookbinding equipment,
such as board shears, presses, stamping
equipment

Arista Surgical Supply Co., Inc.
67 Lexington Avenue
New York, NY 10010
(212) 679-3694
Fax: (212) 696-9046
Knives, handles, and blades;
micro-spatulas

Book Makers International Ltd.
6701B Lafayette Avenue
Riverdale, MD 20737
(301) 927-7787
Fax: (301) 927-7715
Bookbinding supplies, equipment, and
tools; books on bookbinding

Campbell-Logan Bindery, Inc.
212 Second Street, North
Minneapolis, MN 55401-1433
(800) 942-6224
Fax: (612) 332-1313
Japanese bookcloth

Dieu Donne Papermill, Inc.
433 Broome Street
New York, NY 10013-2622
(212) 226-0573
Fax: (212) 226-6088
Handmade paper; books

Harcourt Bindery
51 Melcher Street
Boston, MA 02210
(617) 542-5893
Fax: (617) 451-9058
Bookbinding supplies, equipment,
and tools

Iris Nevins Decorative Papers
PO Box 429
Johnsonburg, NJ 07846
(908) 813-8617
Fax: (909) 813-3431
Marbling supplies, tools; marbled paper.
Reproduces historical patterns.

New York Central Art Supply, Inc.
62 Third Avenue
New York, NY 10003
(212) 473-7705; (800) 950-6111
Fax: (212) 475-2513
Paper of all kinds; bookcloth; books;
general art materials

PaperConnection International
208 Pawtucket Avenue
Cranston, RI 02905
(401) 461-2135
Fax: (401) 461-2135
Papers, mostly Japanese handmades

TALAS
568 Broadway
New York, NY 10002-1996
(212) 219-0770
Fax: (212) 219-0735
Paper; bookbinding supplies, equipment,
and tools; books

INTERNET RESOURCES:

Rag & Bone Bindery
www.ragandbone.com

The Diary Registry
www.diarist.net

Journals and Diaries
207.158.243.119/html/
journals___diaries.html

The Secret Diary
www.spies.com/~diane/
journals.html

Journal Jar Ideas
www.omnicron.com/~fluzby/
sister-share/journal.htm

Writing the Journey
www.writingthejourney.com

Keeping Personal Journals
www.uncg.edu/eng/courses/
mjabrams/101/diary.htm

Metajournals
www.metajournals.com

Just Journaling by Joyce Chapman
www.joycechapman.com/
journal.html

The National Journal Network
www.geocities.com/SoHo/9993/

Journal and Essay Writing
www.poewar.com/links/essay.htm

Conversations Within
www.journalwork.com

Suite 101: Journal Writing
www.suite101.com/welcome.cfm/jour-
nal_writing

Open Pages
www.hedgehog.net/op/

Memoirs, Journals, Diaries, Stories
www.wizard.net/~loiselle/story_2.html

LifeTales
members.tripod.com/karenrager/
ring.html

Diary-L
www.diarist.net/list/

Journal Share
www.onelist.com/community/
journalshare

The Scribe Tribe
www.myplanet.net/bdalporto

Thrive's Online Journal Writing Program
thriveonline.aol.com/serenity.journal/
index.html

Journal Store
www.journalstore.com

BOOKS ON BOOKBINDING:

Bannister, Manly, *Craft of Bookbinding,*
Dover Publications, 1994

Blake, Kathy, *Handmade Books: A Step-by-Step Guide to Crafting Your Own Books,*
Bulfinch Press, 1997

Browning, Marie, *Handcrafted Journals, Albums, Scrapbooks & More,* Sterling, 1999

Doggett, Sue, *Bookworks: Books, Memory and Photo Albums, Journals, and Diaries Made by Hand,* Watson-Guptill, 1998

Feliciano, Kristina, *Making Memory Books by Hand: 22 Projects to Make, Keep, and Share,* Gloucester, Massachusetts: Rockport Publishers, 1999

Golden, Alisa J., *Creating Handmade Books,* Sterling, 1998

Greenfield, Jane, *ABC of Bookbinding: A Unique Glossary with over 700 Illustrations for Collectors and Librarians,* Oak Knoll Books, 1998

Johnson, Pauline, *Creative Bookbinding,*
Dover Publicatons, 1990

Kenzle, Linda Fry, *Pages: Innovative Book Making Techniques,* Krause, 1998

Lewis, Arthur Williams, *Basic Bookbinding,* Dover Publications, 1985

McCarthy, Mary, *Making Books by Hand: A Step-by-Step Guide,* Gloucester, Massachusetts: Rockport Publishers, 2000

Richards, Constance, *Making Books & Journals: 20 Great Weekend Projects,* Lark Books, 1999

Ryst, Marie, *Handmade Books & Albums: An Introduction to Creative Bookbinding,* Linden Publishing, 1999

Shepard, Rob, *Handmade Books: An Introduction to Bookbinding,* Search Press, 1995

PUBLICATIONS ON JOURNALS/JOURNALING:

Personal Journaling
www.journalingmagazine.com

20th Century Women (e-zine)
www.20thcenturywomen.com

CONTRIBUTORS

Rag & Bone Bindery
One Allens Avenue
Providence, RI 02903
info@ragandbone.com
www.ragandbone.com
Bookbinding studio creating hand-bound journals and more.
Established in 1991.
Wholesale only.

Betty Auchard
115 Belhaven Drive
Los Gatos, CA 95032
(408) 356-8224
btauchard@aol.com

Catherine Badot-Costello
20 Purchase Street
Newburyport, MA 01950
(978) 462-5494
marcobadot@compuserve.com

Bruce Barry
337 Adams Street
Milton, MA 02186
(617) 628-8574
www.brucebarry.com
Ceramics instructor and studio manager at the Decordova Museum School, Lincoln, Massachusetts

Laura Blacklow
215 Erie Street
Cambridge, MA 02139
(617) 492-2054

Gary Brown
8 West Mountain Drive
Santa Barbara, CA 93103
(805) 969-6716

Jo Bryant
630 Graceland Drive SE
Albuquerque, NM 87108

Janis Cheek
8621 Hahn Street
Utica, MI 48317

Elizabeth Clark
1505 West Willetta Street
Phoenix, AZ
mussaku@hotmail.com
Proprietor of Mussaku, a shop specializing in handmade books, boxes, and portfolios

Maura Cluthe
4514 Cambridge Street
Kansas City, KS 66103
fragmented@earthlink.net

Juliana Coles
829 San Lorenzo NW
Albuquerque, NM 87107
lovepete@highfiber.com
www.meandpete.com
Exhibiting artist and creator of Sketchbooks, Journals, Art and Beyond classes

Jane Conneen
The Little Farm Press
820 Andrews Road
Bath, PA 18014
(610) 759-5326
lfarmpress@aol.com

Beatrice Coron
372 CPW #20D
New York, NY 10025
beart@idt.net
www.idt.net/~beart
Bookbinder and papercutting artist

Joan Duff-Bohrer
123 Gillis Hill Lane
Salem, NY 12865
(518) 854-9552

Evelyn Eller
71-49 Harrow Street
Forest Hills, NY 11375
eller-rosenbaum@worldnet.att.net

Katy Gilmore
1555 H Street
Anchorage, AK 99501
Author/illustrator of *The Year In Flowers: A Daybook* and other illustrated journals

Wendy Hale Davis
40 Crockett Street
Austin, TX 78704
worldbridger@earthlink.net
Teaches workshops on bookbinding leather inlay

Carol Hamoy
340 East 66th Street
New York, NY 10021

Susan Hensel
6077 Hortzon Drive
East Lansing, MI 48823
(517) 337-8370
booklady@voyager.net

Shireen Holman
14 Dellcastle Court
Montgomery Village, MD 20886
(301) 990-1198
tholman@clark.net

Sherri Keisel
114 Paintbrush Street
Lake Jackson, TX 77566
sherites@aol.com
Teaches workshops integrating lettering, drawing, and painting; bookbinder

Marie Kelzer
P.O. Box 14634
San Francisco, CA 94114
Bookbinder, book repairer, and creator of hand-decorated paste paper

Dorothy Simpson Krause
32 Nathaniel Way
P.O. Box 421
Marshfield Hills, MA 02051
(781) 837-1682
dotkrause@dotkrause.com
www.dotkrause.com
Professor of computer graphics at
the Massachusetts College of Art in
Boston

Bruce Kremer
P.O. Box 2458
Ketchum, ID 83340
bruce@bkremer.com
www.bkremer.com
Teacher, illustrator, artist, and avid
travel journaler

Stephanie Later
201 East 77th Street, Apt. 11F
New York, NY 10021
(212) 249-5330

Roberta Lavadour
48006 Saint Andrew's Road
Pendleton, OR 97801
paper@oregontrail.net
www.papertrails.com
Teaches classes for adults in beginning and intermediate book and
paper arts

L.K. Ludwig
P.O. Box 103
Slippery Rock, PA 16057
(724) 266-5643
lkludwig@home.com
http://victorian.fortunecity.com/
rodin/546/gryphonsfeather
Artist, journaler, and publisher
of Memory & Dream, a journal-
keepers' 'zine

Raphael Lyon
67 Barclay Road
Clintondale, NY 12515
Bookbinder specializing in heirloom gifts

Sally Mac Namara-Ivey
848 East Main Street
Sheridan, OR 97378
(503) 843-5598
sivey@onlinemac.com
Collector of 18th-, 19th-, and
20th-century manuscripts and
ephemera

Peter Madden
109 F Street
Boston, MA 02127
(617) 269-5284
boyauboy@aol.com

Michelle Martinez
309A Girard Boulevard SE
Albuquerque, NM 87106
(505) 268-6156
mischagrace@yahoo.com
Art instructor and writer/editor of
La Fuerza Feminina, a feminist
'zine produced by mixed-race
women

Barbara Mauriello
231 Garden Street
Hoboken, NJ 07030

Jeanne Minnix
6401 Academy Road NE, #69
Albuquerque, NM 87109
jminnix@griffinassoc.com
Art director and graphic designer

Linnea Montoya
2025 Palomas Drive NE
Albuquerque, NM 87110
(505) 265-6874
linnyag@hotmail.com

Teesha Moore
39570 SE Park Street, #201
Snoqualmie, WA 98065

Tracy Moore
39570 SE Park Street, #201
Snoqualmie, WA 98065

Zea Morvitz
P.O. Box 305
172 Highland Way
Inverness, CA 94937
zeamo@svn.net
Book artist and creator of artists'
journals

Maria Pisano
6 Titus Lane
Plainsboro, NJ 08536
(609) 799-3941
mgpstudio@aol.com

Dawne Polis
1348 Mad Tom Road
East Dorset, VT 05253
ddcpolis@vermontel.net

Marilyn Reaves
1260 West 15th Avenue, #6
Eugene, OR 97402
(541) 485-7862
mreaves@darkwing.uoregon.edu
Teaches classes in calligraphy and
design

Raven Regan
4825 Victory Street
Burnaby, B.C., Canada
V5J 155
(604) 433-2759
raven_regan@yahoo.com

Marilyn Rosenberg
67 Lakeview Avenue West
Cortlandt Manor, NY 10567
(914) 737-2052

Val Roybal
208 Edith Boulevard SE
Albuquerque, NM 87102
valr@unm.edu

Julia Sarcone-Roach
Rhode Island School of Design
2 College Street
Box 1689
Providence, RI 02903

Kimberly Schwenk
203 Girard Boulevard SE
Albuquerque, NM 87106
(505) 232-6648
kschwenk@unm.edu

Judith Serebrin
420 Arch Street
Redwood City, CA 94062
(650) 364-1659
serebrin@pacbell.net
Teaches classes for creative writing

Laura Shelby
718 Mountain Road NW, #8
Albuquerque, NM 87102
(505) 842-7383
laura.shelby@mail.ihs.gov

Melissa Slattery
255 South Avenue
New Canaan, CT 06840
wrslattery@snet.net
Teaches classes at the Center for
Book Arts, New York, NY

Cheryl Slyter
26100 Hawthorne Drive
Franklin, MI 48025
(248) 737-1932
slyter@oeonline.com
Teaches bookbinding and calligraphy at the Birmingham Bloomfield
Art Center in Birmingham,
Michigan

Polly Smith
1047 North Lombard Avenue
Oak Park, IL 60302
(708) 524-8194
pilpol@aol.com
Classically trained musician and
self-taught artist

Raymond H. Starr, Jr.
11412 Marbrook Road
Owings Mills, MD 21117
(410) 363-6952
rstarr@research.umbc.edu

Elizabeth Steiner
P.O. Box 60 026
29 Kohu Road
Titirangi, Auckland 1230
New Zealand
steiner@iprolink.co.nz

Ilira Steinman
One Allens Avenue
Providence, RI 02903
(401) 455-3680
ilira@ragandbone.com
www.ragandbone.com
Artist, milliner, and co-owner
of Rag & Bone Bindery,
Providence, RI

Roz Stendahl
630 Huron Boulevard SE
Minneapolis, MN 55414
roslyn.m.stendahl-1@tc.umn.edu
Teaches journal- and book-making
and digital art classes; co-coordina-
tor for the Minnesota Journal
Project 2000

Jason Thompson
One Allens Avenue
Providence, RI 02903
(401) 455-3680
jason@ragandbone.com
www.ragandbone.com
Journaler and owner of Rag &
Bone Bindery, Providence, RI

Yesha Tolo
182 Roger Willimas Avenue
Providence, RI 02907
mattyesha@yahoo.com
Artist, craftsperson, and mom

Kez Van Oudheusden
30 Brooke Street
Clayfield, Australia Q4011
061-7-3862-4074
kez@eis.net.au

Deborah Waimon
1 Cherry Hill Lane
New Milford, CT 06776
Nontraditional printmaker
with works combining encaustic
and collage
(860) 354-7638

Anne Woods
986 Botsford Road
Ferrisburgh, VT 05456
maasalama@hotmail.com
Designer, illustrator, and
textile artist

INDEX

ABOUT THE AUTHORS

The work on pages 12-13, 18-115 originally appeared (in slightly different form) in *Making Memory Books by Hand, 22 Projects to Make, Keep, and Share,* by **Kristina Feliciano**, copyright Rockport Publishers, 1999. Author Kristina Feliciano is a former managing editor of *American Artist* magazine, and a freelance editor for *The New York Post.* She has written on art, photography, and design for numerous trade and news publications, is the editor of the website drummergirl.com and a writer and editor for the New York City-based Happy Mazza Media Company.

The work on pages 14-15, 184-285 originally appeared (in slightly different form) in *Making Journals by Hand, 20 Creative Projects for Keeping Your Thoughts,* by **Jason Thompson**, copyright Rockport Publishers, 2000. Author Jason Thompson is the founder and president of Rag and Bone Bindery in Providence, Rhode Island. The largest hand-bookbinding studio in America, Rag and Bone Bindery creates hand-bound blank books, albums, and journals for the gift and stationery industries. Jason began journal writing in 1986, when he spent a year on the Great Peace March walking from Los Angeles, California, to Washington, D.C. He has been keeping visual journals ever since. He is a book artist, music collector, designer, and webmaster for www.ragandbone.com, and he currently resides in Providence, Rhode Island, with his beautiful wife and two cats.

The work on pages 116-183, 286-293 originally appeared (in slightly different form) in *Making Memory Boxes, Box Projects to Make, Give, and Keep,* by **Barbara Mauriello**, copyright Rockport Publishers, 2000. Author Barbara Mauriello is an artist and conservator who has a bookbinding studio in Hoboken, New Jersey. She teaches bookbinding and boxmaking at the International Center of Photography, The Center for Book Arts, and Penland School of Crafts.